HERMAN MILLER 1940 CATALOG & SUPPLEMENT

GILBERT ROHDE MODERN FURNITURE DESIGN

REFACE BY: LESLIE PIÑA

WITH VALUE GUIDE

4880 Lower Valley Road, Atglen, PA 19310 USA

Library of Congress Catalog Card Number: 98-86919

Layout by Bonnie M. Hensley
Typeset in Bauhaus LT BT/Times New Roman

ISBN: 0-7643-0705-3
Printed in China

Published by Schiffer Publishing Ltd.
4880 Lower Valley Road
Atglen, PA 19310
Phone: (610) 593-1777; Fax: (610) 593-2002
E-mail: Schifferbk@aol.com

In Europe, Schiffer books are distributed by Bushwood Books
6 Marksbury Rd. Kew Gardens
Surrey TW9 4JF England
Phone: 44 (0)181 392-8585; Fax: 44 (0)181 392-9876
E-mail: Bushwd@aol.com

Contents

Preface

Though much has been said about both extremes of modern furniture from the 1920s and 1930s — Art Deco, handcrafted of exotic materials, and industrially designed and produced tubular steel — most people sat, worked, ate, and slept on traditional furniture. Historic styles continued to fill the American home, and the Herman Miller Furniture Company furnished them. Modernism was budding, but it would not blossom until after the war. The 1950s would become the "golden age" of modern furniture. Whether minimalist curvilinear chairs, biomorphic tables, or rectilinear modular case goods, these 1950s designs are regarded as innovative modern milestones. Herman Miller super-designers George Nelson and Charles and Ray Eames have been justifiably credited with many of the twentieth-century classics.

But it was Nelson's predecessor, Gilbert Rohde, who had introduced modern design at Herman Miller in the early 1930s, and had provided each new design until he died suddenly in 1944. By then, Herman Miller had completely phased out the last remnants of its diehard traditional line and had become a leading force in the spread of modernism in the American home.

The 1940 Catalog represents the culmination of Rohde's work through the 1930s, as well as a foundation for many of the "new" designs introduced in the decades that followed. This remarkable 1940 collection bridges the gap between Art Deco and Postwar Modern. It includes both Deco and a stylistic transition that has not been as well documented or understood. Many of Rohde's chairs, case pieces, and tables have a distinctly 1950s look — or perhaps many 1950s designs have a Rohde 1930s look. Rohde's concepts of modular storage and sectional seating revolutionized the contemporary floor plan and prepared the way for its future widespread popularity. His use of plastics and of tubular steel combined with upholstery and/or richly grained woods resulted in lightness and high style without sacrificing comfort or function. Simplicity of design and the choice of materials enabled Herman Miller to mass-produce Rohde's furniture. Elegance became more affordable; utility became more fashionable, and therefore more marketable. A man and a decade transformed the company; a design team and another decade would transform the American interior.

In addition to conceptual parallels between Rohde's designs and those of the 1950s, individual examples can be strikingly similar. When Nelson introduced the renowned 1948 collection and accompanying hardbound art catalog, Rohde was left to rest in peace. Yet, if the 1939 and/or 1940 Herman Miller catalog is compared with a classic mid-century catalog, say 1955/56, it is clear that at least Rohde's spirit continued. A comparison of the catalogs reveals some strong influences.

Compare, for example:

•1939/40: Rohde's 3548 Desk with integrated typing stand and filing drawer and
•1955/56: Nelson's 9569 Desk

•1939/40: Rohde's 3977 Pedestal Desk with elevated top and
•1955/56:Nelson's 9665 model

•1939/40: Rohde's 7000 Series Wall Units and chests propped on rectangular or cylindrical supports and
•1955/56: Nelson's Basic Cabinet Series.

Features of Rohde's 3400 Chest Groupings also show up in the Basic Cabinet Series. Rohde's distinctive cylindrical metal legs on cabinets and tables reappear on Nelson desks. Rohde's 3425 Console Radio with its circle-in-a-square design is reincarnated as Nelson's 4743 Radio Cabinet. Rohde's 7010 Drop Leaf Table returns as Nelson's 4656 Gateleg Dining Table. Rohde's 3770 Brazilian Rosewood Group is echoed in Nelson's Rosewood Group. Rohde's 3979 Table resembles a solid version of Nelson's Platform Bench. Where Nelson uses the bench as legs to support case pieces, Rohde's designs with single-leg supports produced the same effect. Rohde's 3682 Square Back Easy Chair reappears in 1967 as Nelson's Cube Group. There is even a similarity between the famous Noguchi Coffee Table and the biomorphic glass top of Rohde's 3943 Table.

Designers stand on each others shoulders. Rohde had absorbed ideas from the French and Germans in the 1920s, translated them in Zeeland, Michigan, and introduced them to a new world. When Nelson joined Herman Miller as director of design in 1946, and immediately brought Eames on board, they designed an entirely new line of exclusively modern furniture that carried Rohde into the future. Herman Miller popularized modern concepts such as modular seating and storage and flexible design for multiple rooms and functions. Thanks to farsighted collectors and museums, these pieces from the 1950s are among the most familiar and most widely-collected of all modern American furniture — so much so, that Herman Miller has continued to produce or has reintroduced some of them in a collection called Herman Miller for the Home. Though designed by Nelson and Eames, some of these ideas can be credited to Rohde. There is no such thing as total originality of design, so we are content with new interpretations, twists, and connections. Discovering the connections makes the study of design more compelling, and this catalog can help to reveal some of the connections made in the year 1940.

Several items in the 1939 catalog, such as the Mahogany Groups, were dropped from the line in 1940. There were also more than 50 items added in 1940, such as the American Ash Group, the king-size bed, pieces using Lucite and Plexiglas, and a chair upholstered with plastic webbing. A few pieces by other designers, such as 15 modern lamps, plus the last of the traditional line are also in the catalog. The 1940 supplement features about 100 additional new items, including 16 pages of the highly important Paldao Group, with its kidney-shaped and other freeform tables and desks, plus new bentwood and bent plywood chairs.

The catalog and supplement are courtesy of Herman Miller, Inc.

Leslie Piña

The Herman Miller Furniture Company 1940

Hedrich-Blessing Studio

GENERAL INFORMATION

Every Floor Salesman Should Familiarize Himself with the Facts Concerning Herman Miller Modern

"THEY" said Robert Fulton's steamboat would never work. "They" said the automobile would never replace the horse, that man was never intended to fly, that radio was an impractical dream. Even Edison considered the phonograph and motion picture machine little more than interesting toys.

Every forward step in the progress of mankind has been accompanied by the raucous chorus of scoffers.

Today, after a dozen years, the acceptance and permanence of Modern Design is no longer questioned, but it, also, ran the gamut of criticism based upon an unyielding adherence to ancestoral interpretations of form and beauty. Today, the question with which progressive-minded persons are concerned is not: "Is Modern Design good?" Rather is it: "What in Modern Design is good and what is bad?"

Now, as always, the acceptance of artistic expression is determined by the all important factor of good taste. The cycles of civilization show that when the culture of a people is high the acceptance of what is "good" in art is assured. And the reverse is equally true. But what is "good" must result from the creative effort of the artist and the designer — who, after all, are but the products of their eras — and the name of an artist — if that name means anything, is just as important today as ever. Certainly the names of outstanding designers and outstanding manufacturers of furniture are as important today as were names and personalities during the days of Chippendale, Sheraton, Hepplewhite and the Brothers Adam. Oddly enough, since that time and the days of Duncan Phyfe and his contemporaries in this country the name and identification of the furniture designer was lost for a century — completely submerged until — until the development of the Modern Idea. And today in an era of aggressive and ingenious competition the names of the designer and the maker are more important to the buyer than in the past.

Foremost in this present day school of modern design are the names of Gilbert Rohde and Jan Ruhtenberg whose contributions to modern living have been accorded world wide recognition.

Foremost also in a sympathetic appreciation and the manufacture of functional American Modern is the Herman Miller Furniture Company who were among the first to sponsor "designer designed" Modern furniture at a time when "they" said it was but an interesting novelty.

Since that time all the facilities and thinking of the Herman Miller organization has been devoted to the consideration of what in modern design is good and what is not good, what is worthy to survive in the history of furniture design and what should unfeelingly go to the scrap heap.

Today, the modern school of design is as firmly rooted in contemporary culture as any prior school of artistic development. In no sense superficial, it is definitely grounded in the necessities and economies of the modern way of living.

Today, every piece of Herman Miller Modern is either an original Gilbert Rohde or an original Jan Ruhtenberg design — imbued with the spirit of the nation's leading modernists — and as such richly deserving their place in the sun.

HOW THIS CATALOG IS PLANNED

This book is in two sections. The first part is devoted to Modern Design. The second part illustrates the Herman Miller line of Traditional Design.

It will be noted that the Modern is arranged somewhat in the order that would be followed in planning the furnishing of a home. First, beginning with the living room, the desired utilities are considered. Second, the available wall space is figured. Next, the important seating pieces are determined upon and this is followed by a selection of tables and occasional pieces.

MODERN SUITABLE FOR PRACTICALLY ALL HOMES

The House

In order to use modern furniture it is not necessary to have a home designed in the modern style. Modern furniture fits into the apartment house and the majority of small houses. An apartment house is of necessity "modern" and to use 17th and 18th Century furniture and an electric elevator is simply an anachronism that continues because it hasn't been noticed.

Most single family houses do not possess any true historical characteristics and are modern in the sense that they are nothing else. Modern furniture is, therefore, at least as appropriate in these homes as any other type and in most cases more so.

The Room

Herman Miller Modern furniture does not require any architectural setting other than plain flat walls, free from paneling or any other characteristic that is reminiscent of a historical style. Such plain walls are precisely the kind that are found in the majority of homes.

The Grouping Idea

The GROUPING idea is one of the basic features of well designed modern furniture. It is the idea which makes it possible to use the space in your rooms so that they are less crowded even though they provide more utilities.

The idea is simple. Let us take for example the average bedroom. Adequate equipment for a bedroom to be shared by two people requires TWO chests of drawers and a dressing table. These three pieces, together with the bed, require *four separate* walls in the case of old-fashioned furniture. However, very few bedrooms contain four wall spaces of such size and location as to permit the placing of four pieces so that they look well and are in the proper place in the room for convenient use.

The difference of one wall solves this problem. Almost all bedrooms do have three good wall spaces. If, therefore, we can get all the required pieces into the room by using only three walls, we can arrange a room properly.

In the case of the bedroom this is simple. Instead of having two chests of drawers of different sizes and shape, we use *two identical* chests which can be grouped, that is placed together, so as to form one unit, which occupies one wall instead of two.

And in addition, you achieve an entirely new *decorative* effect. One large group of chests gives a decorative center to the room which scattered units never achieve.

Following are diagrams of "before and after" which show how advantage is gained.

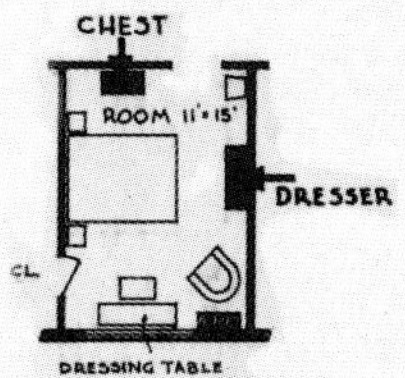

NOT MODERN

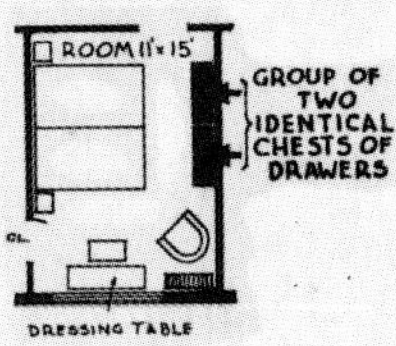

MODERN

An even greater advantage is secured in the case of the living room; especially in the case of the *double purpose* room, the living-dining room, and the one-room apartment.

In a living-dining room of small size it is not possible to have desk space, book space, and dinette chest in the room in *good arrangement* when old-fashioned furniture is used. With modern furniture, however, it becomes simple, and an extremely interesting decorative effect is obtained with the long group of chests.

This is illustrated in the diagrams below:

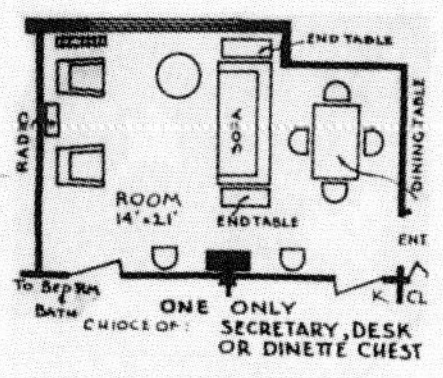

NOT MODERN

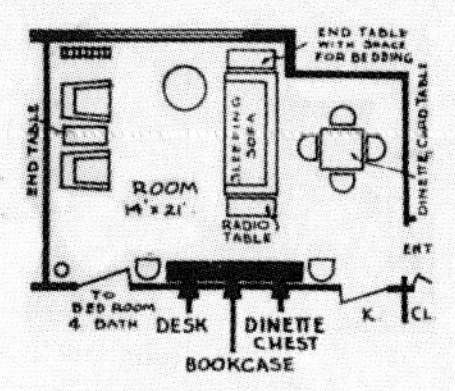

MODERN

A one-room apartment which combines living, dining, and sleeping needs demonstrates the advantages of modern furniture to the fullest extent. One of typical size and shape is shown below. The modern arrangement does everything — all utilities are provided, free floor space remains at the maximum, and the decorative effect is strong and unified.

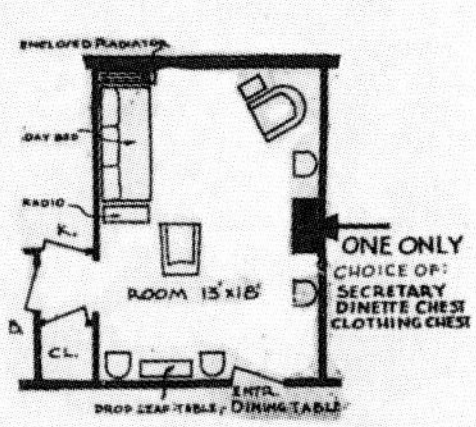

NOT MODERN

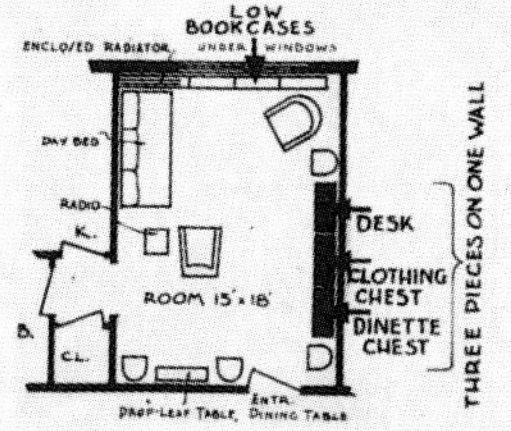

MODERN

LOGICAL SUGGESTIONS (Pointers)

Painting of Walls

The architecture of the room must be considered for the distribution of colors on the walls; a wall with a fireplace, or one containing several doors, or an unbroken wall that is planned as the background for the largest group of furniture should be used as the deciding factor and the rest of the colors apportioned accordingly. A recessed portion of a wall, or an alcove often give an excellent basis for division of color.

Window Treatment

Venetian Blinds or glass curtains are suggested in most modern rooms. It is not well to use both in one room and we recommend that only one or the other be used.

Over-curtains can be used when desired, in either plain, striped or modern figured fabrics. The important thing to remember is that the colors used must harmonize with the rest of the color scheme.

Floors

We suggest a plain colored broadloom carpet as a safe base for all rooms. Scatter rugs can be used over the carpet when desired, provided the colors and designs are in keeping with the rest of the room.

Accessories

The accessory furnishings should be, as in the case of any other furniture, in the same spirit as the furniture, but remember to keep them simple.

Pictures

Pictures are good if the pictures are good. Some of the better magazines now regularly reproduce drawings by good artists. These are perfect for the small pictures when framed in plain narrow wood frames, which can be unfinished wood or bright lacquer, or framed in the adjustable "Braquette" frames.

Plan for Ensemble Effect

Furniture and accessories are not selected primarily for their individual beauty and novelty; but what is of importance is the appearance of the ensemble when completed. The furnished room as *a unit* is what counts.

FURNITURE OF TRADITIONAL DESIGN

Although the market for Modern Design has the greatest sales possibilities for future selling as indicated by the increasing preference for these compact, functional forms and the grace and comfort achieved, there still remains a demand for Traditional styles. To many, due to a variety of reasons, this type of furniture design will remain desirable, and this market cannot be overlooked by any merchant who wants to keep his offerings to the public well rounded.

The Herman Miller line of Traditional design, while by no means as extensive as is the Modern showing, is exceptionally choice. Meticulous attention has been given to the historical verities of form and style and to the minute details of decorative motifs. In every Herman Miller Traditional piece the significance of the period has been faithfully reproduced — the spirit and atmosphere of the era has been captured.

In manufacture, the same standards of construction that identify all Herman Miller products are paramount. Materials, finish, the hidden qualities of fine cabinet work and the apparent evidences of expert craftsmanship welcome the most discriminating inspection.

QUALITY — HIDDEN AND VISIBLE

The making of furniture is a maze of detail. An average dresser requires 332 operations to complete. Two hundred seventy-two of these are done by machinery. Yet these 272 machine operations represent less than 35% of the total labor hours and about 65% of the time allowance is taken by the 60 hand operations. Even in a so-called mass production plant this ratio is practically the same. The price paid for furniture is therefore largely determined by the amount of handwork and the quality of materials used.

The outstanding difference in a cheap piece of furniture and a good one is the handwork. It is better made, better finished, will last longer and be more satisfactory because of the necessary handwork. In the manufacture of Herman Miller furniture the following is standard practice:

Only high grade cabinet woods used.

Fine veneers are selected with care and matched with expert precision.

Curved veneer parts are usually made of eleven plys laid in forms. This assures more permanency and uniformity than four plys on a bandsawed core, which is the customary method.

Flush effects, always an important requisite in pure modern design, are the result of precision machining and careful fitting of long mitres. These are impossible without trained men and good equipment.

Handwork is the only way to properly produce many of the quality earmarks of a piece of furniture. Fitting drawers and corner blocks; preparation of wood for finishing; padding; toning; glazing; distressing; antiquing; and block rubbing the final finish require time and skilled hand craftsmanship.

In the paragraph on upholstering other hidden qualities of Herman Miller furniture are mentioned.

CONCERNING THE FINISH

The efforts of many "hand workmen" combine to produce the Herman Miller finish. From white stock to the final satin glow of the rubbed finish the trained hands of expert finishers add their bit to the built-up finish applied to all Miller furniture.

Color-fast penetrating stains give the depth so necessary to really fine pieces. Carefully applied washcoats protect the cleanliness of the fine veneers while numerous hand sandings prepare the surfaces for their protective coats. Filling is hand-wiped to smooth every pore and then thoroughly dried. Further sizing with the all important hand sand prepares for skillful glazing, padding, toning and shading in order to bring out the true color richness of the woods.

To protect this acquired beauty multiple coats of the finest lacquers are used. Hard drying sealers are applied as a foundation coating with special attention being given to elasticity and check prevention. These pyroxylin coatings have been tested for durability. Sealers are again hand sanded before the application of the first lacquer coating. After the first coat of lacquer has been applied it is thoroughly dried and "nub-sanded" before the second coat is applied. The final coat is thoroughly dried to carefully prepared schedules to insure no shrinkage or blooming of final finish. The backs, drawers, and interior parts are given protective lacquer coats to seal out unwanted moisture and the piece moves on to hand rubbers and polishers.

In the rubbing department, fine pumice and rubbing oil, applied with a felt block, by experienced rubbers, brings out the full beauty of the surfaces, and it is here that training and knowledge permit these finishers to produce the delightful satin smoothness of the truly built-up finish. Miller furniture is COMPLETELY hand-rubbed — not just tops nor fronts nor selected first glance areas. Miller furniture is FINISHED ALL OVER with equal attention, to give lasting beauty and enduring satisfaction to the purchaser. A liberal coating of hard wax which is applied by hand completes the finest finish which can be applied to wood.

FINISHES

In this catalog, the standard finish for each wood in the group is mentioned. Special finishes can be obtained at approximately 15% extra. Different woods can usually be finished in matching colors, although grain effects cannot be made to match.

Pieces are only finished as orders are received. This insures factory fresh pieces. Time required for this is usually two weeks unless pieces are temporarily out of stock, in which case you will be promptly notified.

Wood samples of finishes in which you are interested can be mailed promptly on request.

UPHOLSTERY CONSTRUCTION

The deep seated chairs and sofas are made in only one high grade seven-point construction:

1. Full close-webbed bottom, held to frames by long shank nails (not tacks).
2. Individual tempered steel springs, sewed to webbing four times.
3. Eight no-slip knot tied with Italian twine, and frame edges rounded to avoid cutting twine.
4. All horse hair filling under long staple white cotton.
5. All easy chairs with tight seats double-springed and double-stuffed, to give the maximum comfort of loose cushions and the tailored effect of tight seats.
6. Muslin cover under fabric making a double cover.
7. Only double-dowelled, sound hardwood frames are used; reinforced with substantial hand-fitted corner blocks glued and screwed.

COMBINATION UPHOLSTERY

Two different cover materials may be used on DEEP ARM CHAIRS. Combination upholstery is not recommended on small chairs.

Division of the Fabrics

A number of different ways of making the combination can be used, and the method necessary varies with the design of the chair, but the simplest and safest way is to:

Use the DARKER shade on the ENTIRE ARMS (inside, top, front and outside) and the ENTIRE BACK OF BACK and the LIGHTER shade of color on the INSIDE OF BACK, TOP OF SEAT, and FRONT OF SEAT.

GENERAL PRINCIPLES OF COMBINATION

A — Combinations of two shades of the same colors are always good and generally are to be preferred to combinations of two different colors.

B — Combinations of two different colors are usually undesirable, except that *white, grey* and *black* combine well with almost any color.

C — Combinations of *solid color* fabric with a *pattern fabric* of the same or different shade of the same color are particularly good.

D — Combinations of a plain *flat color weave* with a fabric of pronounced texture, but same color, are good, but never combine a dainty dressy fabric such as satin or rayon rep with a rough heavy fabric.

E — Combinations of two different weaves of *pattern goods* are bad.

F — Combinations of one plain and one pattern material can be used, but in that case keep the dominant color of the patterned fabric the same color as that of the plain fabric. Use plain fabric on arms and patterned fabric on seat and inside back.

Stripes are usually best horizontal on the back and same direction on the seat.

Never combine two different patterned goods.

G — Combinations of *lacquered* and *soft* fabrics are good. Use lacquered goods on the *arms*, soft goods on the *seat and back*. Such combinations look good if made with lacquered and soft fabrics of the same color, but they can also be made with a difference in shade or color. Do not use lacquered fabrics on seats and backs which have a lot of flex as the coating of the fabric will crack.

H — WELTING — No blanket rule can cover all cases but it is usually best in the case of combination upholstery to make all welts the color of the *dark* cover material. In any event use only one color of welts throughout. Do not use lacquered fabric for welts, especially on seats and backs.

UPHOLSTERY FABRICS

A wide selection of upholstery fabrics in nine grades and a variety of colors is available. When requesting sample swatches, be sure to state customer's color preference. Muslin prices include the covering of the piece with your fabric if you wish to send in your own cover. Upholstery is done on a custom basis; that is, the frames are carried in stock and upholstered to order. Therefore, orders for upholstered pieces are not subject to cancellation.

INTERIOR DESIGN SERVICE

If you desire suggestions as to room arrangements, colors, and accessories, please send a rough floor plan giving important dimensions, the placement of windows, doors, and radiators, and state any special utilities that are desired in the room.

5

Hedrich-Blessing Studio

Hedrich-Blessing Studio

THE WALNUT LIVING - DINING GROUP

This group includes all pieces needed for:

LIVING ROOM
COMBINATION LIVING-DINING ROOM
ONE-ROOM APARTMENTS
DINETTES AND BREAKFAST ROOMS
CONVENTIONAL DINING ROOM
LIBRARY OR DEN
PROFESSIONAL OFFICE

THE CHESTS and BOOKCASES in the group are developed on the **grouping principle** first introduced for American use by Gilbert Rohde in 1932, and represent the last and final development resulting from years of experience with this type of furniture, so that they provide the maximum of usefulness and flexibility together with fine lines and proportions. These units are planned in several sizes for various purposes as explained below.

All chests of the same height and depth can be grouped in a straight line. All chests of equal height can be grouped around a corner, even though depth of chests on wall is different from depth of chests on the adjoining wall.

WOODS — Wood is American Walnut Veneer, with some solid Walnut parts on outside surfaces. Inside of open compartments are also veneered with Walnut.

The chest group and the flat top desk have fine line inlays of White Holly.

One series of small occasional tables have solid White Maple legs as noted.

Drawer interiors are White Oak.

FINISHES — A choice of two finishes is available; **Natural** and **Dark.** The **Natural** finish gives the true color of unfinished Walnut, a light grey-brown, entirely free from the usual yellowish color imparted by finishing materials, yet is accomplished without any unnatural bleaching of the wood. This is a unique achievement in finishing. It is called Miller Grey Walnut.

The open compartments of chests and cases will always come finished "Dark" when the "Natural" finish is ordered. The interiors of these compartments are almost entirely hidden when books or other objects are in place, and the Dark finish here gives a better effect.

The **Dark Finish** is a conventional dark stained walnut, inside of open compartments being the same as the outside.

Small tables having Maple legs show special notation for finishes in the photographs.

THE CHESTS — Desk, Utility Chest, Deep Bookcase.

GROUPING — Can be used singly or any number can be grouped in any order desired. They can also be arranged on two adjoining walls so that they form a group that turns a corner. Corner fillers make this possible. If desired a group of these 16-in. deep chests can be used on one wall, joined to a bookcase (or group of bookcases) only 11 in. deep. The corner fillers take care of the difference in depth. Diagrams that follow explain this in detail. Width of these chests — 40 in.

LEGS — All three of these chests are available in a choice of two types of legs.

Type "L" leg is unique in furniture design. It is made of a tube of **Lucite** or clear transparent plastic with a delicate satin finish brass cap at the lower end. The transparent leg gives an effect of lightness as the furniture seems to be suspended in air. Leg "L" is 5 in. high, resulting in a finished chest height of 39 in.

Type "S" leg is of wood, also 5 in. high. This is in the skid design, but is unique in that it tapers toward the bottom, giving a lighter effect than the usual skid.

Two of the chests, the bookcase and the utility chest, are available in a third type of base, solid wood, 2 in. high. This results in a finished chest height of 36 in. This base cannot be used on the desk as the level of the writing surface would then be too low. This base is Type "F."

PULLS — Drawer and door pulls are of **Plexiglas,** another crystal-clear transparent plastic, that becomes almost invisible and gives beautiful unbroken wood surfaces on the fronts of the cases, catching only jewel-like reflections of light.

No. 3970-L Chest Desk
W 40 D 16 H 39
Closed

Three Shallow Drawers.

Convenient space for portable type-writer here in upper part of interior.

Letter file drawer, on double extension slides.

Leg "L"

No. 3970-L Chest Desk
W 40 D 16 H 39
Open

ALL WALNUT

No. 3942 Table
No. 3958 Chair

No. 3972L Utility Chest
No. 3971L Bookcase
No. 3970L Wall Desk
No. 90 Corner Filler

No. 3956 Chair

No. 3972-L Utility Chest
W 40 D 16 H 39

THIS CHEST can be used for glassware or general storage in living rooms, as buffet or dinette chest in combination living-dining rooms, as chest of drawers in a bedroom, or for storage of both dining equipment and clothing in a one-room apartment.

No. 3971-L Bookcase
W 40 D 16 H 39

ALL WALNUT

No. 3950 Chair
No. 3974 Bookcase
No. 3975 Cabinet

No. 3975-F Low Cabinet
W 36 D 11 H 24
2 Doors with Adjustable Shelf Inside

No. 3974-F Low Bookcase
W 36 D 11 H 24

Either of the cases shown above can also be placed on top of either of the deep chests or desks. This can be done, however, only if the lower piece is used singly, as the low chest and bookcase are not the same width as the high deep chests.

CORNER GROUPING

All chests of the **same height** can be grouped around a corner regardless of the depth of the chests by the use of the Corner Filler. The Filler is attached to one case by metal plates screwed to the back. Diagrams showing how they can be used are shown below.

No. 90 Filler to be attached to Nos. 3970, 3971, 3972 Cases.
T 16 x 16 H 34

No. 91 Filler to be attached to Nos. 3970, 3971, 3972, 3973 Cases.
T 10¾ x 16 H 34

No. 92 Filler to be attached to No. 3973 Case
T 10¾ x 10¾ H 34

No. 93 Filler to be attached to Nos. 3974, 3975 Cases
T 10¾ x 10¾ H 22

No. 3976 Bookshelves
W 54 D 15 H 28

ALL WALNUT

No. 3977 Desk
W 48 D 24 H 29

The No. 3977 Desk shown above has two drawers in the right pedestal. The top drawer is a partitioned drawer and the bottom drawer is a large vertical file also partitioned. The left pedestal has a Pull-out at the proper height for typing. It also has three trays. Removal of the lower tray provides storage space for the typewriter.

Double top provides extra space for correspondence and working papers.

For large desks, tables, and files for executive and professional offices, please send for photos and information. We have a very efficient series for that purpose.

No. 3973-S Bookcase
W 40 D 11 H 39

No. 90 Corner Filler
W 16 D 16 H 34

No. 3973 Bookcases
No. 3977 Desk
No. 3965 Chair

ALL WALNUT LIVING-DINING PIECES

No. 3978 Console Dining Table
Closed
L 54 D 20 H 29½

No. 3978 Console Dining Table
Open
L 54 D 40 H 28¼

No. 3998 Table
T 30 x 30 Closed
T 39½ x 30 Open
H 29

No. 3947 Lamp Table
L 32 W 15 H Lower Part 19
Upper Part 24
Hardware — Statuary Bronze

No. 3997 Drop Leaf Table
Closed
T 36 x 13 H 29

No. 3997 Drop Leaf Table
Open
T 67 x 36 H 29
Legs — Statuary Bronze Pulls — Plexiglas

The standard finish on the tables illustrated below is Miller Grey Walnut. If this finish is specified for the first four tables they will be supplied with white bleached legs and Miller Grey tops. If legs are wanted in the same Miller Grey color as the top be sure to specify it.

These tables can also be finished in American Walnut, a darker and browner color.

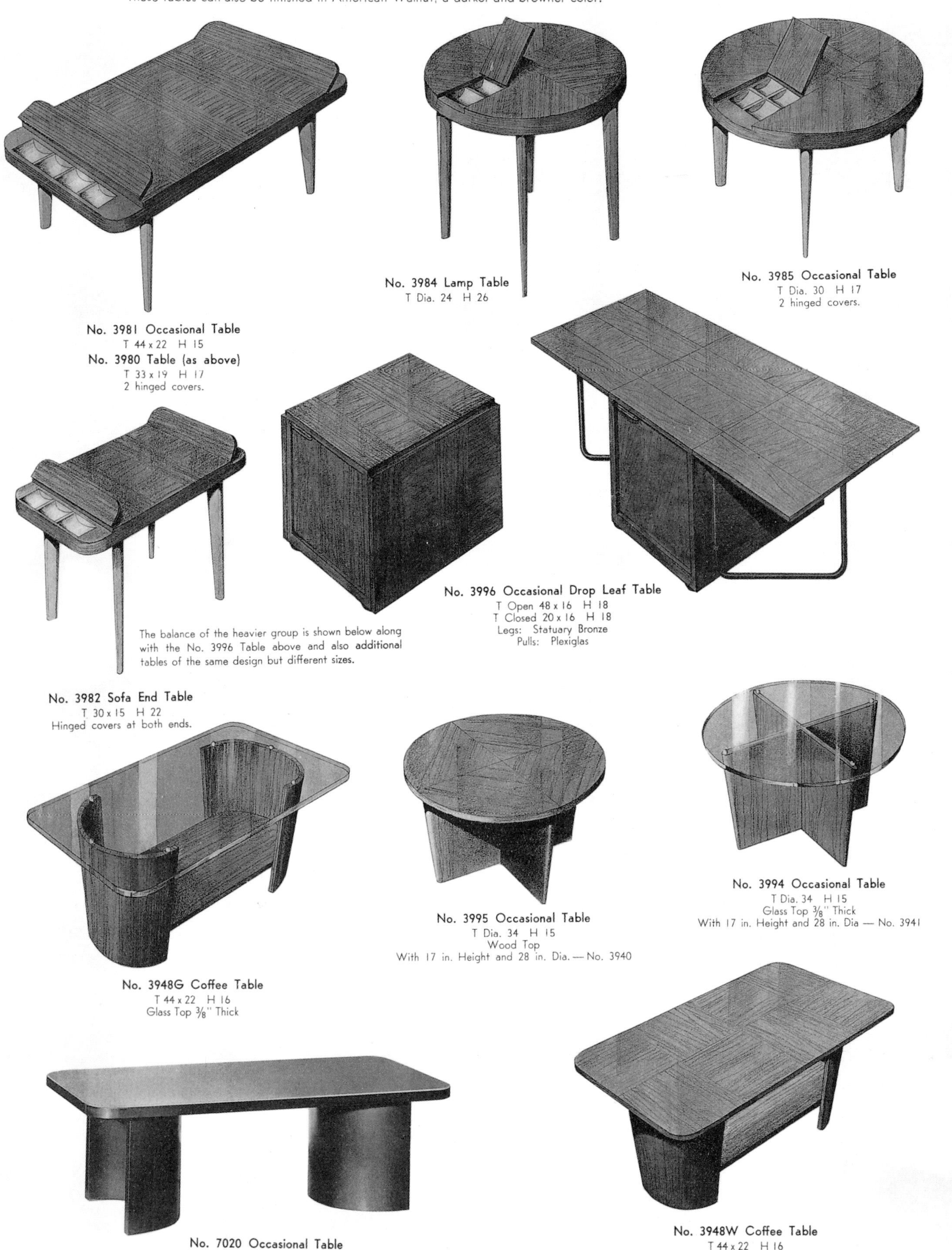

No. 3981 Occasional Table
T 44 x 22 H 15
No. 3980 Table (as above)
T 33 x 19 H 17
2 hinged covers.

No. 3984 Lamp Table
T Dia. 24 H 26

No. 3985 Occasional Table
T Dia. 30 H 17
2 hinged covers.

No. 3996 Occasional Drop Leaf Table
T Open 48 x 16 H 18
T Closed 20 x 16 H 18
Legs: Statuary Bronze
Pulls: Plexiglas

The balance of the heavier group is shown below along with the No. 3996 Table above and also additional tables of the same design but different sizes.

No. 3982 Sofa End Table
T 30 x 15 H 22
Hinged covers at both ends.

No. 3994 Occasional Table
T Dia. 34 H 15
Glass Top 3/8" Thick
With 17 in. Height and 28 in. Dia — No. 3941

No. 3995 Occasional Table
T Dia. 34 H 15
Wood Top
With 17 in. Height and 28 in. Dia. — No. 3940

No. 3948G Coffee Table
T 44 x 22 H 16
Glass Top 3/8" Thick

No. 7020 Occasional Table
L 44 W 22 H 14 1/4

No. 3948W Coffee Table
T 44 x 22 H 16

No. 3944 Table No. 3935 Sofa

LUXURY GROUP OF OCCASIONAL TABLES

These have a ¾-in. thick plate glass top with polished edges. The legs are LUCITE tubes; Lucite is a sparkling, colorless, transparent plastic. The legs have satin finished brass caps at the lower end, and are attached to the glass top with heavy decorative machine turned brass fittings. This is a unique design by Gilbert Rohde of a luxury seen heretofore in custom designed pieces at many times the present prices.

The tables are shipped "knocked down," but the legs can be attached to the top without the use of tools.

No. 3942 Table
28 Dia. H 17½

No. 3943 Table
L 29¾ W 18 H 17½

No. 3944 Table
W 44 D 22 H 15½

No. 3945 Table
D 34 H 15½

13

Hedrich-Blessing Studio

Hedrich-Blessing Studio

AMERICAN ASH GROUP

The new American Ash group on the following pages was designed to make well-planned and well-equipped rooms for that large group of people who want good Modern furniture at moderate prices. American Ash is a rugged textured wood. A variety of finishes can be applied without destroying its character. Four marvellous colors are available: Honey, Autumn, Woodrose, and Acorn. Samples of any of these will be sent on request. This custom finishing enables you to plan individual color schemes for your clients at a very reasonable price. Notwithstanding these prices, the quality is, of course, equal to anything else we make.

The following utilities can be supplied in one living-dining room from this group of pieces:

Seating for 10.

Dining for 10.

Reading — 17 feet of bookshelf space.

Space for radio, phonograph, telephone.

Utility desk for study, home-work, writing, typing and sewing.

Storage for dishes, glassware, silver, files and records, phonograph albums, hobby materials, projector and films, games, portable typewriter and portable sewing machine.

Matching bedrooms are the No. 3630 shown on pages 54 and 55, and the No. 4010 on pages 66 and 67.

No. 4020 All-In-One Chest
L 60 D 18 H 39

No. 4021 Top Unit
L 52 D 13 H 29

No. 4019 All-In-One Chest
L 60 D 18 H 39

The All-in-one Chest is a combination of several wall units and, therefore, makes an excellent basis from which to start the planning of a living or dining room, or a combination living-dining room. The piece serves as a buffet when equipped with a sliding tray such as the No. 4020. A top unit can be added which will do duty as a china or a breakfront bookcase. When the drop lid compartment is equipped with a pigeonhole it serves as a desk. One of the open spaces can be equipped with a radio panel, housing the speaker and chassis behind it. These spaces are also suitable for storing books, etc. One of the drawers is equipped with a velvet lined silver tray.

This chest provides storage for linens, dishes, phonograph record albums, etc.

AMERICAN ASH GROUP

No. 4028 Bookcase
L 52 D 13 H $32\frac{1}{2}$

The No. 4019 All-In-One Chest can be grouped well with the following units illustrated below: Nos. 4022, 4024, 4025.

No. 4024 Left Bookcase
L 30 D 13 H 39

No. 4026 Drop Lid Desk
L 30 D 13 H 39

No. 4027 Corner Cabinet
Overall $33\frac{1}{2}$ x $26\frac{1}{2}$ H 39
Wall Size $21\frac{3}{4}$ x $21\frac{3}{4}$

No. 4022 Bookcase
L 30 D 13 H 39

No. 4025 Right Bookcase
L 30 D 13 H 39

AMERICAN ASH GROUP

No. 4038 Dining Table
Top Closed 50 x 34
Top Open 86 x 34
Height 29

No. 4036 Arm Chair
W 24 D 24 H 32½
¾ Yard

No. 4039 Drop Leaf Extension Table
Top Closed 20 x 36
Top Open 78 x 36
Height 29

No. 4039 Table
Extended

The No. 4039 Table is a drop-leaf unit that occupies very little space against a wall as a console. It can quickly be made into a 36 x 36 in. table and can be extended from that into several sizes up to 78 in. When extended to that length, while not absolutely rigid, it is sufficiently so to provide dining space for eight to ten guests.

No. 4035 Side Chair
W 20 D 24 H 32½
¾ Yard

AMERICAN ASH GROUP

No. 4023 Desk
L 49 D 24 H 29
Closed

No. 4023 Desk
Open

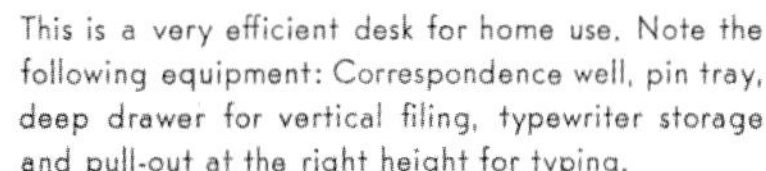

This is a very efficient desk for home use. Note the following equipment: Correspondence well, pin tray, deep drawer for vertical filing, typewriter storage and pull-out at the right height for typing.

No. 4040 Coffee Table
L 33 D 18 H 16½

No. 4044 Coffee Table
Dia. 29½ H 15½

No. 4043 Lamp Table
L 28 D 14 H 26

No. 4045 Lamp Table
Dia. 22 H 27

WALNUT LIVING ROOM GROUP

No. 929 Movable Drawer Unit
L 15 D 26 H 24¼

No. 928 Desk Table
L 48 D 27 H 29

The No. 928 Desk Table has drawers on both sides so that two can use the table as a desk at the same time. The No. 929 Movable Drawer Unit can be used at either end of the desk or pulled out to serve as a stand for the typewriter. It also serves as an occasional piece.

No. 925 Bookcase
L 38 D 12 H 37
With Glass Doors it is No. 927

The No. 925 Bookcase can be furnished with sliding glass doors and is then designated as No. 927. When equipped with doors as shown in the interior on page 20 it is designated as No. 926.

No. 922 Coffee Table
L 28 D 16 H 18

The low cost Walnut group on this and the next two pages was designed by Jan Ruhtenberg especially for the New York World's Fair. The House of Vistas in the Town of Tomorrow was the outstanding exhibit of true American Modern at the Fair and it was entirely furnished from this group. The design is utterly simple. Precision mitred flush corners and edge veneering give real character. Comparatively speaking, there are few pieces in this group but because of their multi-purpose planning, every room in the house except the kitchen can be efficiently furnished. The wood is Walnut and the standard finish is Dawn Grey. The interiors illustrated were taken in the House of Vistas at the Fair.

WALNUT DINING GROUP

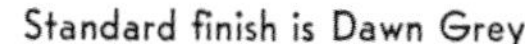

Standard finish is Dawn Grey

No. 937 Chair
Overall Size 20 x 17 H 34
1 Yard 50" Material

No. 935 Table
L 54 D 28 H 28

No. 938 Buffet
L 38 D 18 H 37

No. 936 Table
L 28 D 28 H 28
Serves as the Extension for No. 935 Table and also as a Serving or Utility Table

No. 939 Cabinet
L 19½ D 18 H 37
Fits with No. 938 Buffet
Useful as a Silver Chest, Music Cabinet or Phonograph Record Case

WALNUT BEDROOM GROUP

No. 940 Bed
4' 6" or 3' 3"

No. 941 Dressing Table
L 39 D 17½ H 26
Center Mirror 15 x 20
Wing Mirror 6 x 20

Frosted glass bottom in cosmetic compartment removable for easy cleaning.

No. 944 Chest
L 38 D 18 H 37

No. 943 Chest
L 38 D 18 H 29

The No. 943 and No. 944 Chests can be used as twin chests in the living room as well as in the bedroom.

Hedrich-Blessing Studio

Below is a corner of a one-room apartment. It shows the No. 3440 box spring frame fitted with a box spring and mattress covered in suitable upholstery fabrics for daytime use as a sofa and night time as a bed. Other views of this room are shown on page 24.

WALL UNITS IN EAST INDIA LAUREL

The standard finish is natural, a grayish Walnut color — All cases 41 in. high

No. 3425 Desk
Open
L 32 D 15 H 41

No. 3425 Desk
Closed
L 32 D 15 H 41

No. 3432 Bookcase
L 32 D 15 H 41

The lower part of the No. 3425 Desk serves a number of utilities. The right has shelves. Lower Deep Drawer for Vertical File.

No. 3450 Chair
No. 3465 Chair
No. 3425 Desk
No. 3436 Rest-on Shelf
No. 3437 Utility Cabinet

WALL UNITS IN EAST INDIA LAUREL

No. 3426 Utility Chest
Closed
L 32 D 15 H 41

No. 3426 Utility Chest
Open
L 32 D 15 H 41

No. 3635 Chest of Drawers
L 32 D 15 H 41

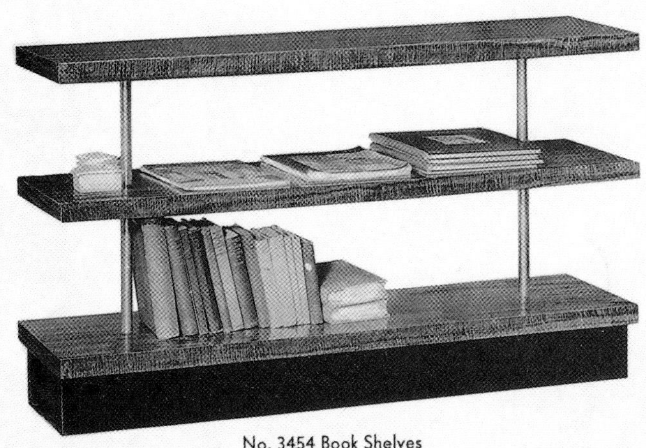

No. 3454 Book Shelves
L 54 D 15 H 30

No. 3425 Console Radio
W 24 D 15 H 30

No. 3437 Utility Chest
L 24 D 15 H 30

No. 3435 Rest-on Shelf
L 24 D 15 H 11

To build up No. 3425 Radio or No. 3437 Utility Chest to the height of the 41 in. wall units.

The Nos. 3634, 3633, and 3632 Bookcases, shown in the interior at the left in that order, are made as an individual group and do not line up with the other Laurel Bookcases. The two end Bookcases can also be used to make up a wall group and any of them can be used singly.

They are 32 in. wide, 11 in. deep, and 39 in. high.

LAUREL LIVING - DINING TABLES

EAST INDIA LAUREL

No. 3435 Console Dining Table
Closed
L 56 D 16 H 28

No. 3435 Console Dining Table
Open
L 56 D 32 H 28

No. 3568 Extension Table
Open
Laurel
T 30 x 60

No. 3568 Extension Table
Closed
Laurel
T 30 x 30

LAUREL OCCASIONAL PIECES

EAST INDIA LAUREL

Hedrich-Blessing Studio

No. 3440 Box Spring Frame
Inside Measurement for Spring 74 x 33

No. 3441 Box Spring Frame
Inside Measurement for Spring 74 x 39

No. 3548 Desk
Closed
T 44 x 22 H 29

No. 3548 Desk
Open with Portable Typewriter
The Pull-out is at the proper height for typing. The drawers are planned for convenient and orderly filing. The two lower trays can be removed to make storage space for the typewriter.

No. 3427 Flat Top Desk
L 44 D 19 H 29
Glass Top Only

No. 3425 Day Bed End
L 46 D 15 H 24

LAUREL OCCASIONAL PIECES

EAST INDIA LAUREL

No. 3740 Chair Grouping Table
L 32 W 29 H 19
E. I. Laurel

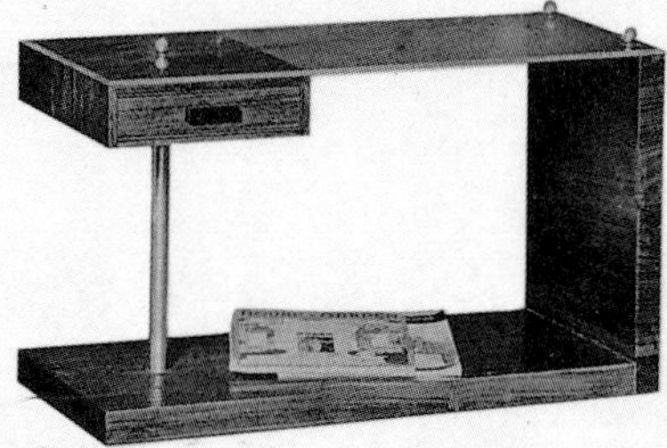

No. 3428 Coffee Table
L 32 D 14 H 18

No. 3552 Coffee Table
T 24 x 24 H 16

No. 3562 Occasional Table
Laurel
B 32 Dia. H 16½

No. 3550 Occasional Table
T 24¾ Dia. H 19

No. 3554 Occasional Table
T 18 x 18 H 16

No. 3549 Sofa End Table
T 30 x 13 H 20½

No. 3431 Sofa End Table
L 14 D 33 H 19

No. 3461 Sofa End Table
L 33 D 15 H 20½

No. 3460 Sofa Radio
W 33 D 15 H 20½

No. 3434 Radio Table
L 17 D 17 H 21

No. 3549A Lamp Table
T 30 x 13 H 20½

No. 3460 Table
No. 3461 Radio
No. 3457 Chairs

27

Hedrich-Blessing Studio

Hedrich-Blessing Studio

COMBINATION CHAIRS

No. 3700 Straight Unit Chair
Overall size 22 x 35½
H 30 Seat Height 16
3 Yards

No. 700 Arm
Overall size 32 x 14 x 3
1 Yard

No. 3701 Corner Chair
Overall size 35½ x 35½
H 30 Seat Height 16
5 Yards

No. 3704 Double Sector Chair
Overall size 92 x 35½
H 30 Seat Height 16
7¼ Yards
Curve of back on 60" Radius

No. 3708 Single Sector Chair
Overall size 46 x 35½
H 30 Seat Height 16
4⅓ Yards
Curve of back on 60" Radius

No. 3722 Two-Seater Sofa
Overall size 45 x 36
H 32 Seat Height 16
4½ Yards

No. 3703 is the Three-Seater matching above
Overall size 66 x 36
H 32 Seat Height 16
6 Yards

No. 3702 Round Corner Chair
Overall Size 50 x 35½
H 30 Seat Height 16
4 Yards

The above chairs all fit together so that they can be arranged in a variety of shapes and give as much seating space as the room permits.

COMBINATION CHAIRS

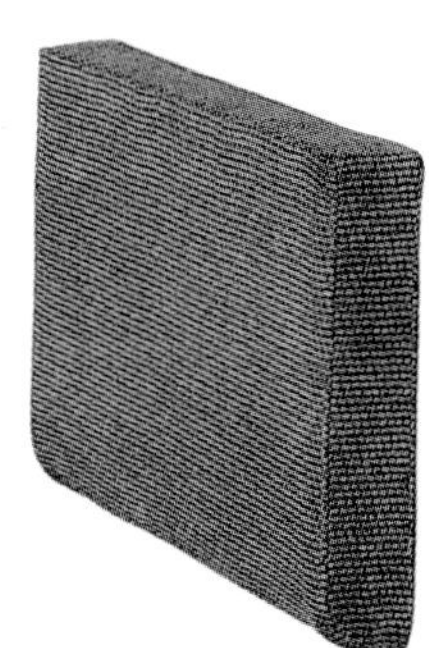

*No. 258 Sofa Arm
1⅓ Yds. 50-in. Material

No. 3457 Flat Chair
22 x 31
Seat H 16 B H 32
2⅔ Yds. 50-in. Material

No. 3459 Corner Chair
31 x 31
Seat H 16 B H 32
4 Yds. 50-in. Material

No. 257 is the two-seater sofa matching these chairs. Its length is 46 in., 4 yds., 50 in. material.

*No. 357 Armless Sofa
L 68
6 Yds. 50 in. Material

*Use in combination with No. 3457 and No. 3459 Chairs.
Specify right or left (facing piece) when ordering Arm.

SLEEPING SOFA

No. 3580 Sleeping Sofa
Overall size 36 x 78 Depth 33 without pillows
22 with pillows
Between Arms 74
12½ Yds. 50-in. Material

No. 3580 Sofa
Open

In its normal position the seat slopes for comfortable sitting. Simply swinging over a lever hidden between the arm and the seat, levels the seat for sleeping. You then have a bed for emergency sleeping which is most luxurious because an inner spring unit is used over the usual webbed and double cone spring foundation.

Hedrich-Blessing Studio

SOFAS

No. 3556 Sofa
With Welts
Overall Size 80½ Between Arms 71½ D 22
14 Yards 50 in. Material

No. 3546 Sofa
With Welts
Overall Size 57 Between Arms 47 D 22
10 Yards 50 in. Material

No. 546 Sofa
Without Welts 10½ Yards

Fabrics with patterns or pronounced pattern in weaves, such as herringbone, not suitable for use on the outside of above pieces, if welts are desired. With such materials specify the number that calls for plain back.

No. 5272 Sofa
Birch
Overall Size L 76 D 30
Between Arms L 66 D 22
10 Yards 50 in. Material

No. 3727 Reception Seat
Overall Size 26 x 49
Seat H 18 H 33
Between Arms 46
2½ Yards 50 in. Material

SOFAS

No. 3935 Sofa
Overall Size L 66 D 39 H 30
Seat H 16
6 Yards

Matching chair is No. 3958 on page 35.

Tufts are built for permanency and, therefore, the sofa is not as comfortable at first as it will be after some use.

Correction — No. 3935 Sofa is made with truncated cone-shaped legs as illustrated in the room scene on opposite page (Page 33).

No. 3706 Sofa
Overall size 70 x 32
Between Arms L 66 H 27
7 Yards

A comfortable sofa giving ample room to recline full length, yet occupying a minimum of floor space.

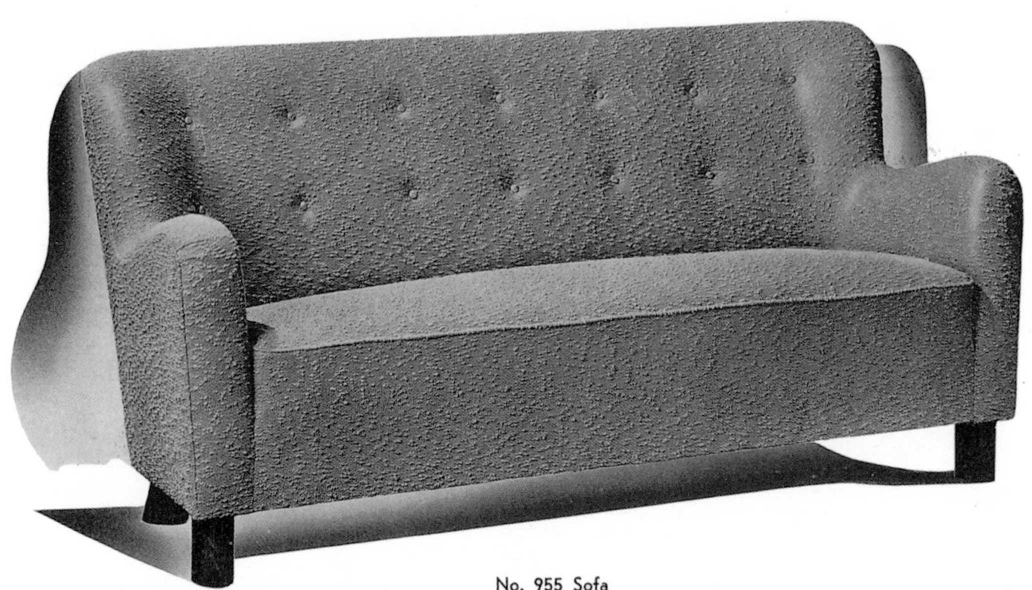

No. 955 Sofa
Overall Size 72 x 30 H 31½
Between Arms 62
8 Yards 50 in. Material

Another space-saving sofa. It is a Danish type. Note the arms and back all contribute to the comfort and relaxation of the occupants. Our tailored tight seats have loose cushion comfort because of a special double spring construction.

SOFAS

No. 4041 Sofa
L 71 D 36 H 29½
Seat Height 17
10 Yards 50 in. Material

For matching chair see page 38.

The above illustration shows down-filled cushions. To get a tailored effect with equal comfort, specify moulded airtex cushions.

Hedrich-Blessing Studio

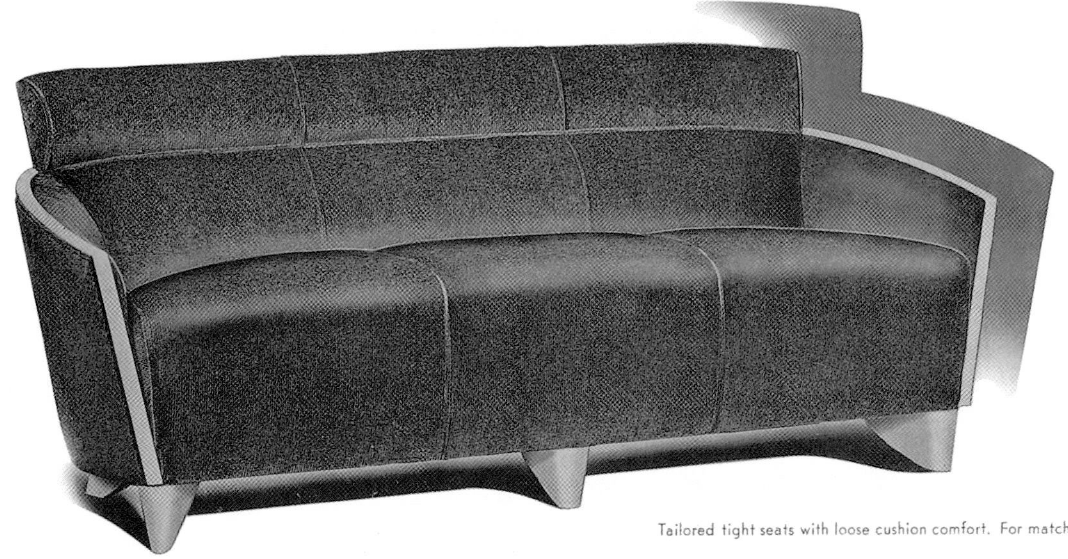

No. 4042 Sofa
L 77 D 32 H 29
Seat Height 17
9½ Yards 50 in. Material

Tailored tight seats with loose cushion comfort. For matching chair see page 38.

Photo courtesy Good Housekeeping Studio

Hedrich-Blessing Studio

EASY CHAIRS

No. 3951 Easy Chair
W 29 D $37\frac{1}{2}$ H 30
Seat Height 16
3 Yards 50 in. Material
White Maple Frame
and Dark Legs

No. 3450 Arm Chair
Overall Size 27 x 39
Between Arms 20 H 33
3 Yards 50 in. Material
Bentwood Arms

No. 952 Ottoman
W 26 D 26 H 16
$1\frac{2}{3}$ Yards

No. 3958 Easy Chair
Overall W 26 D 39 H 30
Seat H 16
4 Yards
Also furnish this chair with Bentwood Arms as No. 3952

No. 3950 Easy Chair
W 38 D 37 H 29
Seat Height 16
5 Yards 50 in. Material
A comfortable Chair no matter in what
position you may be sitting

EASY CHAIRS

No. 3681 Square Back Easy Chair
Overall Size $32\frac{1}{2}$ x 45
Between Arms $22\frac{1}{2}$ H $29\frac{1}{4}$
$5\frac{1}{4}$ Yards

A comfortable chair for the rangy, long-legged fellow.

No. 3445-W Lounge Chair
Overall size 33 x 40
Between Arms 22 H 33
$4\frac{1}{2}$ yards 50" material

No. 3453-W Ottoman
Overall size 20 x 20 H 14
$1\frac{1}{2}$ yards 50" material

Hedrich-Blessing Studio

No. 3451 Bentwood Chair
Overall size 24 x 29
Between Arms 22 H 27
2 yards 50" material

No. 3317 Chair
Overall Size 29 x 33
Between Arms 22 H 31
4 Yards 50 in. Material

EASY CHAIRS

No. 3688 Barrel Back Easy Chair
Overall size 30 x 34½
Between Arms 22 H 31
5 Yards

No. 3784 Round Back Easy Chair
Overall size 36 x 33
Between Arms 22 H 27
5 Yards

No. 3689 Easy Chair
Overall Size 26 x 34
Between Arms 22 H 30
2½ Yds. 50-in. Material

No. 3685 Open Metal Arm Easy Chair
Overall size 28 x 33½
Between Arms 21 H 30
3⅓ Yards

No. 956 Chair
Overall Size 30 x 27 H 31½
Between Arms 22
4 Yards 50 in. Material

See page 32 for matching Sofa

No. 945 Chair
Overall Size 23 x 30 H 28
1½ Yards 50 in. Material

This is a bent plywood frame. It also makes a very good utility chair for either outdoors or indoors, when the frame is covered with jute webbing only, in a checkerboard effect.

No. 4030 Chair
W 25 D 31 H 29½
Seat Height 17
4 Yards 50 in. Material

The above chair is regularly furnished with airtex rubber diaphragm back and airtex molded cushion.

No. 3685 Chairs
No. 3740 Chair Grouping Table

EASY CHAIRS

No. 4032 Chair
W 31 D 32 H 29
Seat Height 17
5 Yards 50 in. Material

No. 4031 Chair
W 27 D 36 H 29½
Seat Height 17
4½ Yards 50 in. Material

No. 3683 Round Back Chair
Overall size 28¼ x 28½
Between Arms 22 H 27
3¾ Yards

See page 33 for matching Sofas for above two Chairs

No. 3705 Twin Grouping Chair
Overall size 26 x 32
Between Arms 22 H 27
3⅓ Yards

No. 3445 Chair — Page 36
No. 3453 Ottoman — Page 36

No. 726 Open Arm Wing Chair
Overall Size 28 x 27
Between Arms 24 H 38
Seat Height 17
4⅔ Yards
Birch — any finish

No. 730 Open Arm Chair
Overall Size 25 x 24
Between Arms 19 H 37
Seat Height 17
3 Yards
Birch — any finish

No. 727 Occasional Chair
Overall Size 26 x 23
Between Arms 20 H 35
Seat Height 17
1½ Yards
Birch — any finish

No. 728 Club Chair
Overall size 34 x 31
Between Arms 21 H 33
Seat Height 18
4½ Yards
Birch

No. 782 Circular Table
T 20 x 20 H 27½
Pine

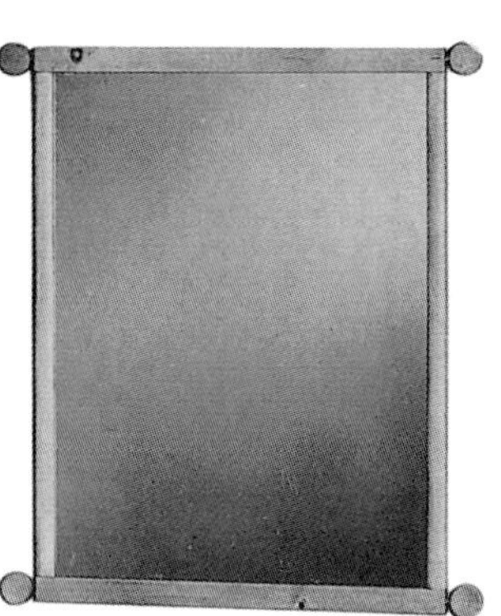

No. 721 V. Mirror
P 24 x 32
Pine

No. 783 Coffee Table
T 27 x 27 H 18½
Leather Top
Pine

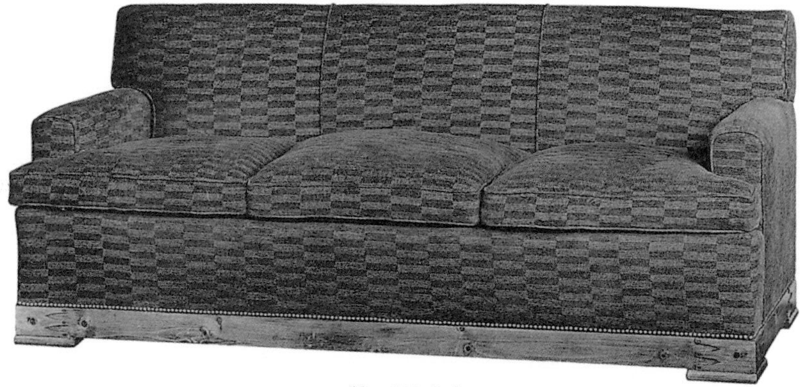

No. 729 Sofa
Overall size 80 x 34
Between Arms 69 H 33
Seat Height 18 10 Yards
Pine

No. 786 Shadow Box Mirror
P 34 x 26
Pine

DESK, BEDROOM AND DINING CHAIRS

Key for Modern Pull-up Chairs: A — Desk Chairs, B — Bedroom Chairs, D — Dining Chairs

No. 930 Arm Chair
Overall Size 25½ x 23½ H 33
Between Arms 22½
1⅓ Yards
A

No. 3954 Bench
W 19 D 21¾ H 20
⅚ Yard
B

No. 3447 Arm Chair
W 25 D 28 H 33½
2½ Yards
A — B

No. 937 Chair
Overall Size 20 x 17 H 34
1 Yard
B — D

No. 4080 Ottoman
Overall Size 24 x 15 H 18
2 Yards
B

No. 3956 Chair
W 26 D 26 H 30
2 Yards
A — B

No. 4090 Chair
Overall Size 19½ x 20 H 33
1½ Yards
All Mahogany or All Walnut
B — D

No. 3323 Ottoman
Dia. 18 H 17
1½ Yards
B

No. 362 Ottoman
Dia. 21 H 18
2 Yards
B

No. 4091 Arm Chair
Overall Size 21½ x 20 H 33
Between Arms 18
1½ Yards
All Mahogany or All Walnut
B — D

Our chair frames, unless otherwise specified, are Birch which is one of the strongest and finest cabinet woods for chair work. It is perhaps excelled only in this respect by Walnut, and Birch has the distinctive advantage in that it can be finished in practically any desired color.

DESK, BEDROOM AND DINING CHAIRS

For key see page 40

No. 3725 Side Chair
W 20 D 24 H 33½
1⅓ Yards
A—D

No. 3726 Arm Chair
W 24 D 24 H 33½
1⅓ Yards
A—D

No. 5208 Side Chair
W 19½ D 19 H 31½
1 Yard
A—B—D

No. 3969 Arm Chair
W 23 D 22 H 31
¾ Yard
A—B—D

No. 3665 Chair
W 18 D 21 H 31
1 Yard
A—B—D

No. 5209 Arm Chair
W 23 D 19 H 31½
1 Yard
A—B—D

No. 3470 Chair
W 19 D 18 H 32
⅔ Yard
A—B—D

No. 3955 Bench
W 18½ D 25 H 19
⅔ Yard

No. 3957 Vanity Chair
W 19 D 24 H 25¼
1⅓ Yards
B

No. 3471 Chair
W 19 D 18 H 32
1½ Yards
A—B—D

Our chair frames, unless otherwise specified, are Birch which is one of the strongest and finest cabinet woods for chair work. It is perhaps excelled only in this respect by Walnut, and Birch has the distinctive advantage in that it can be finished in practically any desired color.

DESK, BEDROOM AND DINING CHAIRS

For key see page 40

No. 3960 Chair
W 20 D 22 H 31
5/6 Yard
A—B—D

No. 3961 Arm Chair
W 24 D 22 H 31
5/6 Yard
A—B—D

No. 3962 Chair
W 20 D 22 H 31
1 1/3 Yards
A—B—D

No. 3963 Arm Chair
W 24 D 22 H 31
1 1/3 Yards
A—B—D

No. 3965 Arm Chair
W 24 D 22 H 31
2 Yards
A—B

No. 3966 Chair
W 20 1/2 D 24 1/2 H 32
1 1/2 Yards
A—D

Specify on order: buttons or channel back.

No. 3967 Arm Chair
W 24 1/2 D 24 1/2 H 32
1 1/2 Yards
A—D

Our chair frames, unless otherwise specified, are Birch which is one of the strongest and finest cabinet woods for chair work. It is perhaps excelled only in this respect by Walnut, and Birch has the distinctive advantage in that it can be finished in practically any desired color.

DESK, BEDROOM AND DINING CHAIRS

For Key see page 40

No. 4035 Chair
W 20 D 24 H $32\frac{1}{2}$
¾ Yards 50 in. Material
Birch B — D

No. 4080 Ottoman
Overall Size 24 x 15 H 18
2 Yards 50 in. Material

No. 4036 Arm Chair
W 24 D 24 H $32\frac{1}{2}$
¾ Yards 50 in. Material
Birch
B — D

No. 764 Arm Chair
Size 18 x 15 H $33\frac{1}{2}$ Seat Height $17\frac{1}{2}$
Brown, or Natural Webbing
Birch
Can also be made with Plastic Webbing
B—D

No. 763 Chair
Size 18 x 15 H $33\frac{1}{2}$
Seat Height $17\frac{1}{2}$
Birch
B—D

No. 4080 Dresser Mirror
Size 29 x 35

No. 3622 Desk
L 32 D 17 H 30
Walnut

No. 3323 Ottoman
See page 40

FORMAL DINING GROUP No. 3725

MAIDOU BURL AND MAHOGANY

No. 3725 Table
T Closed 40 x 68 H 29
T Open 40 x 96
Maidou Burl and Mahogany
3 Apron Fillers 40 x 10

No. 3726 Arm Chair
W 24 D 24 H $33\frac{1}{2}$
$1\frac{1}{3}$ Yards

For additional Dining Chairs see pages 40, 41, 42, 43

No. 3725 Side Chair
W 20 D 24 H $33\frac{1}{2}$
$1\frac{1}{3}$ Yards

FORMAL DINING GROUP No. 3725

MAIDOU BURL AND MAHOGANY

No. 3725 Buffet
I 21 x 72 H 33
Brazilian Rosewood Base
Cork-lined Glassware Trays

No. 3966 Side Chair
W 20½ D 24¼ H 32
1½ Yds. 50-in. Material
Also: Specify on order Button
or Channel Back

No. 3725 China
T 15½ x 34 H 58
Maidou Burl and Mahogany
This piece has Brazilian Rosewood Base.

No. 3725 Server Chest
T 16½ x 36 H 33
Maidou Burl and Mahogany
This piece has Brazilian Rosewood Base.
Two of these in combination make a good Buffet unit.

No. 3967 Arm Chair
W 24½ D 24¼ H 32
1½ Yds. 50-in. Material
Also: Specify on order Button
or Channel Back

FORMAL DINING GROUP No. 3321

WALNUT WITH CHROME BASES

No. 5209 Arm Chair
W 23 D 19 H $31\frac{1}{2}$
1 Yard

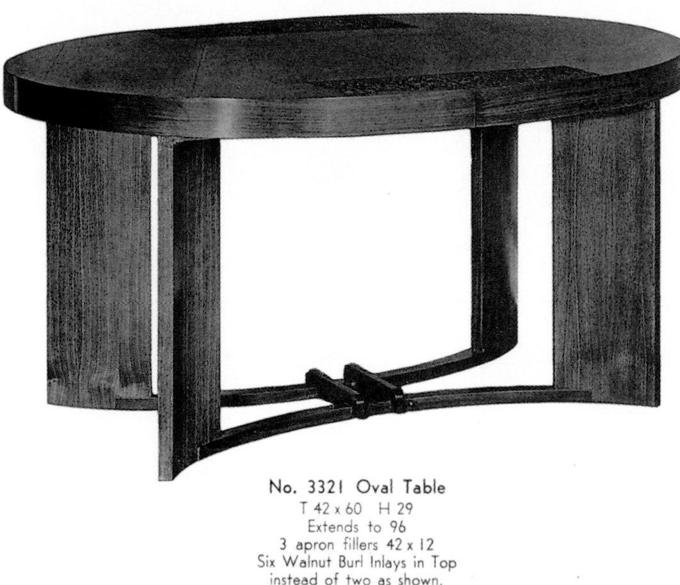

No. 3321 Oval Table
T 42 x 60 H 29
Extends to 96
3 apron fillers 42 x 12
Six Walnut Burl Inlays in Top
instead of two as shown.

No. 5208 Side Chair
W $19\frac{1}{2}$ D 19 H $31\frac{1}{2}$
1 Yard

For additional Dining Chairs see pages 40, 41, 42, 43

FORMAL DINING GROUP No. 3321

WALNUT WITH CHROME BASES

No. 3321 Buffet
T 66 x 17 H 35
Cork lined Glassware Trays

No. 3961 Arm Chair
W 24 D 22 H 31
5/6 Yard

No. 3321 Serving Cart
T 15 x 30
Also matches groups No. 3725 and No. 3979
A good Utility Piece for Living Rooms

No. 3960 Chair
W 20 D 22 H 31
5/6 Yard

No. 3321 China
T 14 x 36 H 52

ALL WALNUT DINING ROOM

No. 3979 Table
T 70 x 34½ H 30
Closed

No. 3979 Table
T 102 x 34½ H 30
Open
Self Container Slide

This table has a new feature developed by Mr. Rohde, its designer. Contained in the top itself are two extra leaves matching the block design which rest and lock on pull-out slides. It is a real improvement over the old time refectory table.

No. 3966 Chair
W 20½ x 24½ x 32
1½ Yards
Specify Button or Channel back

No. 3967 Arm Chair
W 24½ D 24½ H 32
1½ Yards
Specify Button or Channel back

ALL WALNUT DINING PIECES

No. 3979 China
T 36 x 14 H 50
All Walnut
Plexiglas Pulls

No. 3979 Server
T $34\frac{1}{2}$ x $17\frac{1}{4}$ H 30
All Walnut

This server fits with the dining table as an extension. It also is ideal as a console or a lamp table.

No. 3321 Serving Cart
T 15 x 30

No. 3979 Buffet
T 60 x $18\frac{1}{2}$ H 32
All Walnut
Plexiglas Pulls

This buffet has cupboard space at each end for linens and china. The top drawer is partitioned and lined with velvet for silver. The pulls on this piece and the china are clear, sparkling Plexiglas.

FORMAL DINING ROOM

The pieces in this group are all in the generous sizes of Traditional dining rooms so that they can be used in the large sized dining rooms of the older homes.

Designed by John Gartman.

No. 4091 Table
Top Closed 42 x 62
Top Open 42 x 86
H 29
Two 12 in. Apron Fillers

No. 4090 Server
L 44 D 18 H 30
Also a useful Living Room Piece

No. 4090 Buffet
L 60 D 20 H 33
Closed

FORMAL DINING ROOM

No. 4091 Arm Chair
Overall Size $21\frac{1}{2}$ x 20 Between Arms 18 H 33
$1\frac{1}{2}$ Yards 50 in. Material
All Mahogany or All Walnut

No. 4090 China
L 39 D 17 H 70
Beveled Glass in China Top

No. 4090 Buffet
Open
L 60 D 20 H 33
Note the Tray Fronts Trimmed with Mouldings

No. 4090 Side Chair
Overall Size $19\frac{1}{2}$ x 20 H 33
$1\frac{1}{2}$ Yards 50 in. Material
All Mahogany or All Walnut

This group is available in either Paldao or Prima Vera.

The Prima Vera is usually furnished in a Harvest Mahogany color but can also be bleached to a very pale shade.

Paldao is a Philippine wood with easy moving grain. Finished in a dark Walnut color, considerable depth in the wood grain is revealed. Paldao can also be finished in a light grey color. Pulls are transparent Lucite.

No. 3624 BEDROOM GROUP

WHITE ACER AND BLACK WALNUT

No. 3624 Dresser
No. 3625 Dresser
No. 3784 Chair

No. 3624 Left (facing) Dresser
Walnut and White Acer
B 43 x 18 H 36

No. 3625 Right (facing) Dresser
Walnut and White Acer
B 43 x 18 H 36

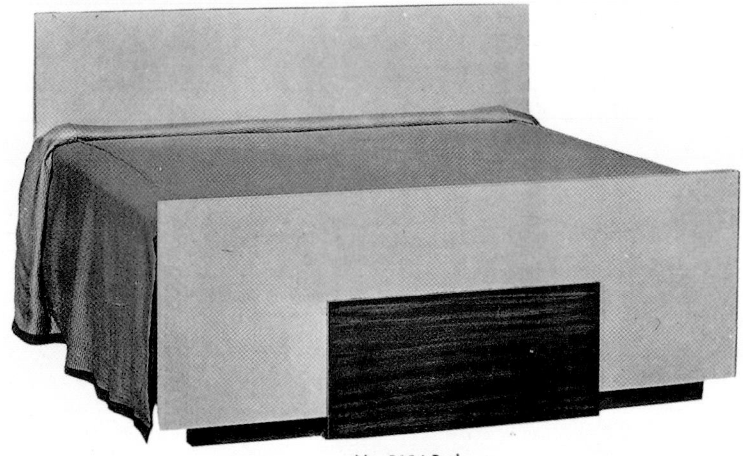

No. 3624 Bed
Walnut and White Acer
W 4 ft. 6 in. or 3 ft. 3 in.

No. 3624 Bedside Table
Walnut and White Acer
B 16 x $12^1/_2$ H 27

53 **No. 3624**

BEDROOM GROUP

WHITE ACER AND BLACK WALNUT

TRANSPARENT CATALIN KNOBS

No. 3624 Vanity
No. 3323 Ottoman

For Bedroom Pull-up Chairs see pages 40, 41, 42, 43.
For Easy Chairs for the bedroom see pages 35, 36, 37, 38.

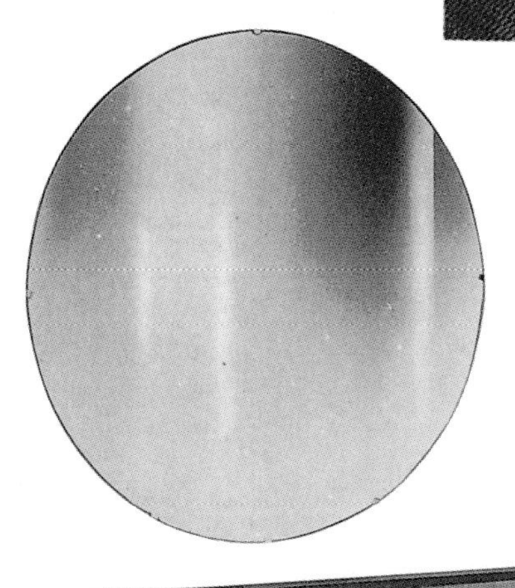

No. 3624 Vanity
Walnut and White Acer
B 52 x 16 H 28 P 32 Dia.

No. 362 Ottoman
Dia. 21 H 18
2 Yards

No. 3950 Easy Chair
W 38 D 37 H 29
Seat Height 16
5 Yds. 50-in. Material

No. 3630 [54]
BEDROOM GROUP

NATURAL STRAIGHT STRIPED WHITE ASH

No. 3317 Chair
Overall size 29 x 33
Between Arms 22 H 31
3½ Yards 50-in. Material

No. 3630 Dresser
Natural Straight Stripe White Ash
B 40 x 18 H 38
P 28 Dia.

No. 3630 BEDROOM GROUP

NATURAL STRAIGHT STRIPED WHITE ASH
A GROUP OF BASIC SIMPLICITY

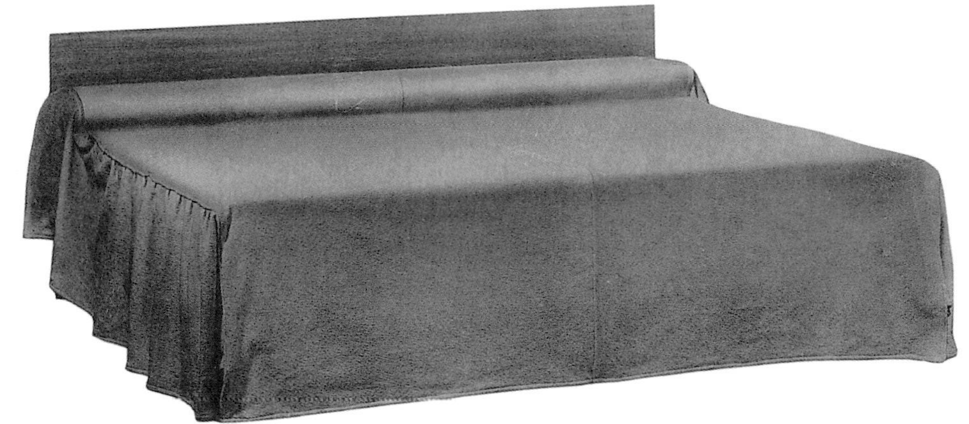

No. 3631 Bed
6' 5" Wide with Seng Twin Type Frames which swing out
Headboard Height 32

Ash is a clean rugged textured wood available in four colors: Honey Ash, Autumn Ash, Woodrose Ash, and Acorn Ash. Honey Ash is the most popular finish.

See pages 14 to 17 for other Ash pieces.

Pulls and edges of footend are of brown imitation leather. Bases are dark.

No. 3631 Bed — 6' 5" wide — Equipped with Seng twin type frames which swing out readily for making the bed. The twin mattresses can be covered with individual spreads or one overall spread as shown.

This twin type bed can be used with other bedroom groups in the line.

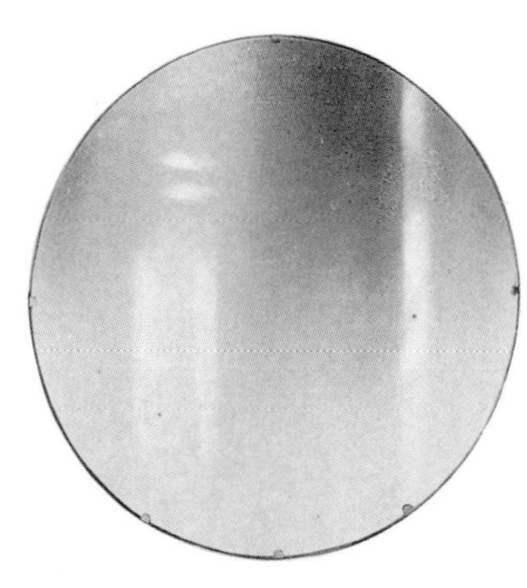

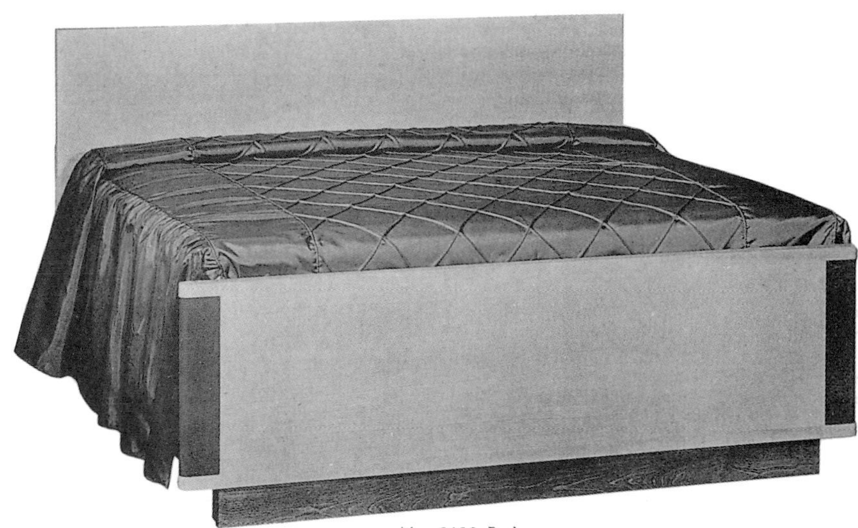

No. 3630 Bed
Natural Straight Stripe White Ash
4 ft. 6 in. and 3 ft. 3 in.

No. 3630 Vanity
Natural Straight Stripe White Ash
B 50 x 16 H 27
P 36 Dia.

See page 40, 41, 42 for Chair and Benches

No. 3630 Bedside Table
Natural Straight Stripe White Ash
B 14 x 11 H 24

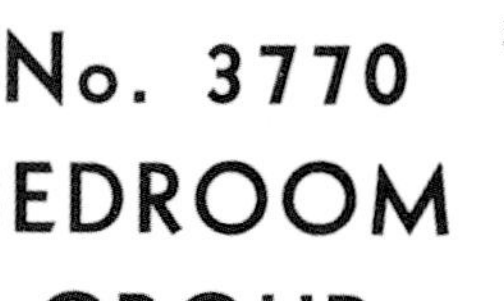

No. 3770 BEDROOM GROUP

BRAZILIAN ROSEWOOD
MAHOGANY INLAY

20 x 64 in. Mirror
No. 3770 Dresser Bases
No. 3784 Chair

No. 3454 Easy Chair
Overall size 31 x 30 H 29
3 Yards

No. 3770 Bedside Table
Brazilian Rosewood
T 14 x 16 H 27

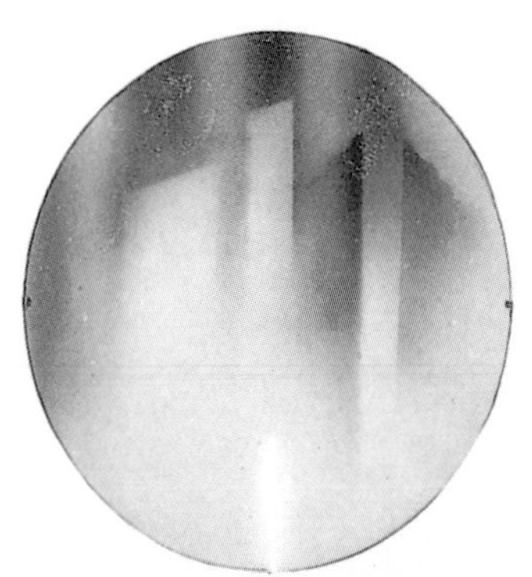

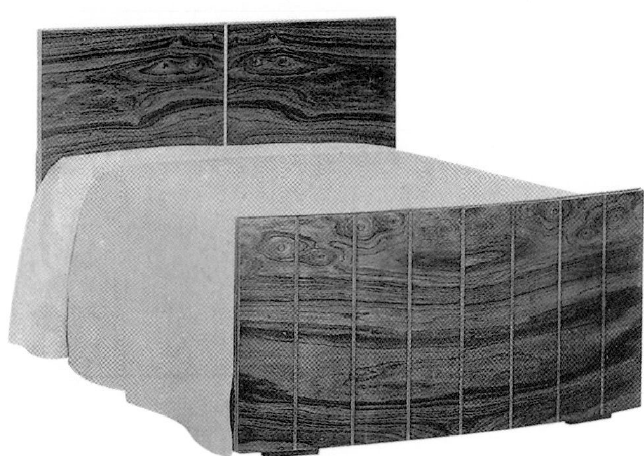

No. 3770 Bed
Brazilian Rosewood
4 ft. 6 in. or 3 ft. 3 in.

No. 3770 Dresser
T 46 x 19 H 34

No. 3770 BEDROOM GROUP

BRAZILIAN ROSEWOOD
MAHOGANY INLAY

No. 3770 Vanity
No. 3323 Ottoman

For bedroom Pull-up Chairs see pages 40, 41, 42, 43
For Easy Chairs for the bedroom see pages 35, 36, 37, 38

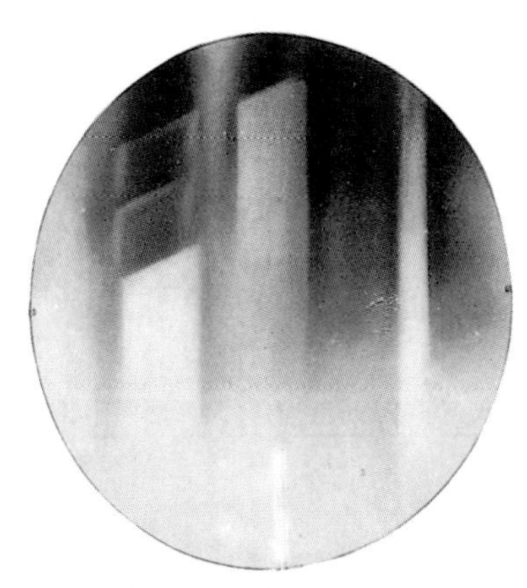

No. 362 Ottoman
Dia. 21 H 18
2 Yards

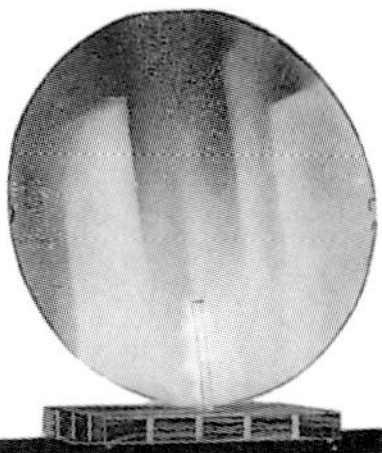

No. 3770 Portable
Brazilian Rosewood
T 9 x 11 1/4
P 18 Dia.

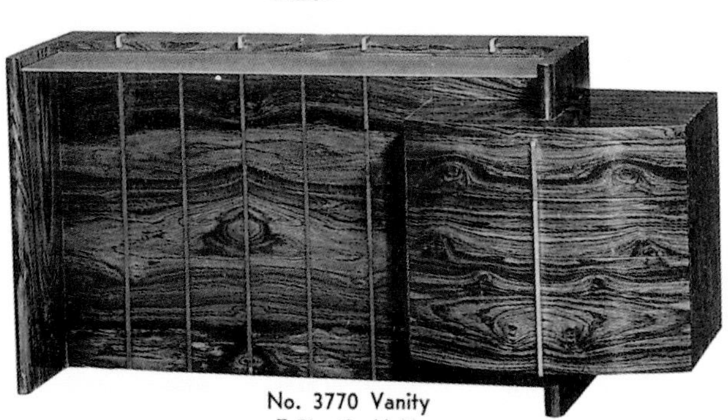

No. 3770 Vanity
T 56 x 18 H 26
Plain Round Mirror 36 in. diameter

CHROME TRIM

No. 3770 Chest
Brazilian Rosewood
T 18 x 34 H 42

No. 3773 BEDROOM GROUP

58

MACASSAR EBONY AND QUILTED MAPLE

No. 3773 Dresser Bases
20 x 54 in. Mirror

No. 3773 Portable
T 11¼ x 9
P 18 Dia.

For bedroom Pull-up Chairs see pages 40, 41, 42, 43
For Easy Chairs for the bedroom see pages 35, 36, 37, 38, 39

No. 3773 Chest
Macassar Ebony and Quilted Maple
T 18 x 33 H 42

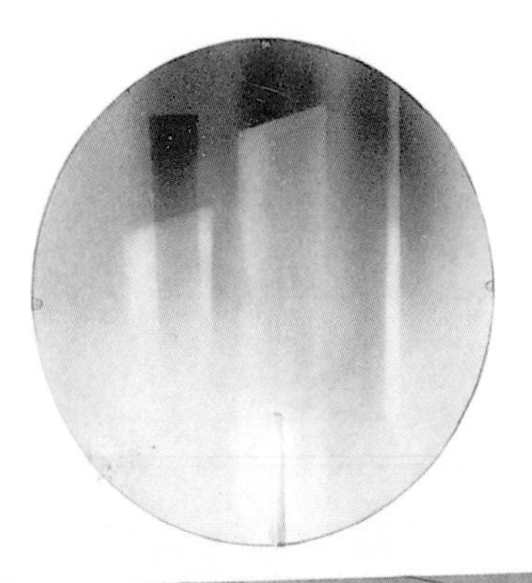

No. 3773 Dresser
Macassar Ebony and Quilted Maple
T 18 x 46 H 34
P 32 Dia.

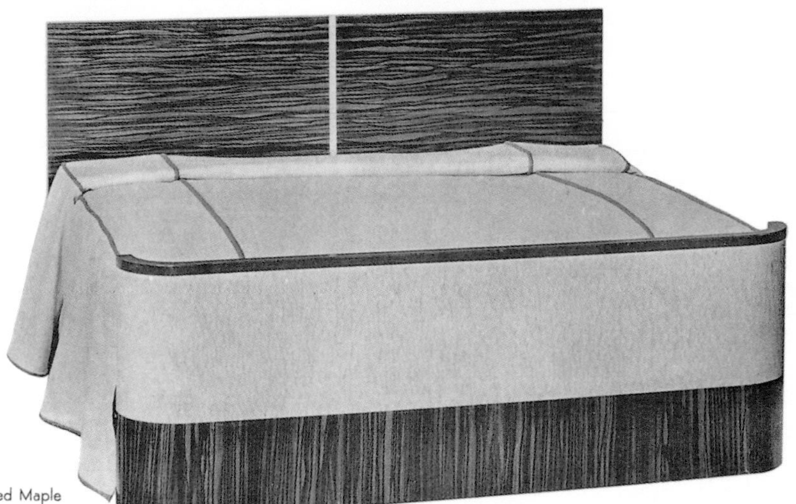

No. 3773 Bed
Macassar Ebony and Quilted Maple
4 ft. 6 in. or 3 ft. 3 in.

59

No. 3773 BEDROOM GROUP

MACASSAR EBONY AND QUILTED MAPLE

No. 3774 Dressing Table
No. 362 Ottoman

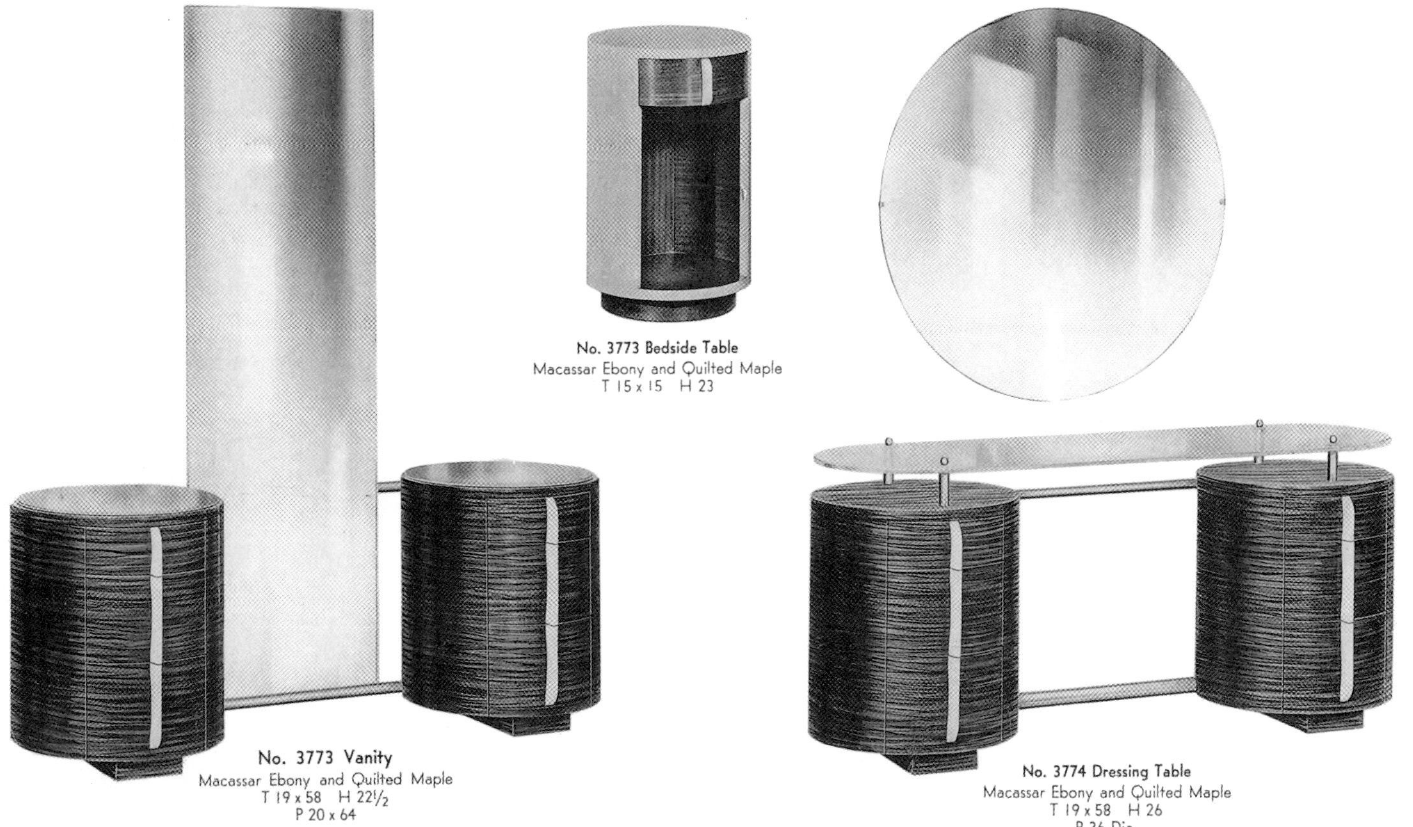

No. 3773 Bedside Table
Macassar Ebony and Quilted Maple
T 15 x 15 H 23

No. 3773 Vanity
Macassar Ebony and Quilted Maple
T 19 x 58 H 22½
P 20 x 64

No. 3774 Dressing Table
Macassar Ebony and Quilted Maple
T 19 x 58 H 26
P 36 Dia.

No. 3930 BEDROOM GROUP

ALL WALNUT
OR
ALL MAHOGANY

20 x 54 in. Mirror
No. 3930 Dresser Bases

For bedroom Pull-up Chairs see pages 40, 41, 42, 43
For Easy Chairs for the bedroom see pages 35, 36, 37, 38, 39

No. 3930 Bedside Table
T 11 x 15 H 26
Mahogany

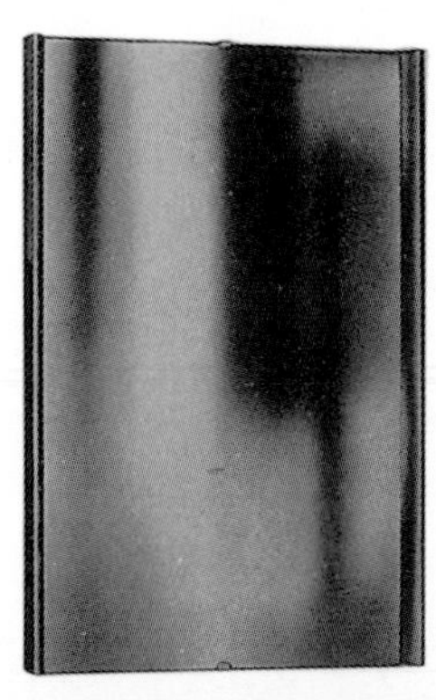

No. 3930 Bed
4 ft. 6 in. and 3 ft. 3 in.
Mahogany

No. 3930 Dresser Base
L 48 D 19 H 33

Dresser Mirror
32 x 20

No. 3930 BEDROOM GROUP

ALL WALNUT
OR
ALL MAHOGANY

No. 3930 Vanity
No. 3955 Bench

Woods: Walnut with Bleached Maple Pulls
Mahogany with either Bleached or Dark Pulls

No. 3956 Chair
W 26 D 26 H 30
2 Yds. 50-in. Material

No. 3955 Bench
W 18½ D 25 H 19
⅔ Yd. 50-in. Material

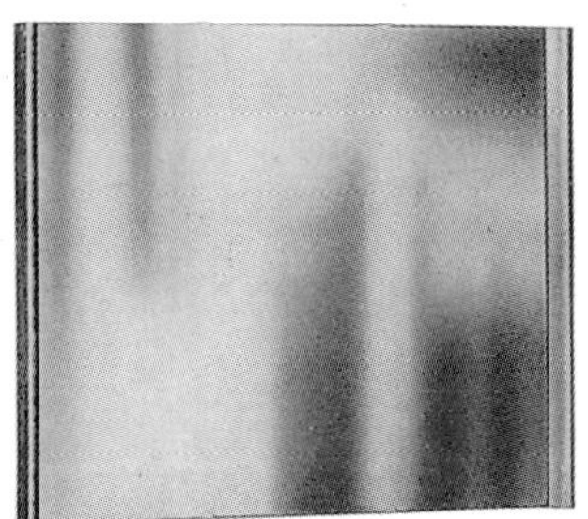

No. 3930 Chest
B 19 x 33 H 46
Mahogany

No. 3930 Vanity Base
L 48 D 18 H 27
Vanity Mirror
29½ x 24

No. 3910 BEDROOM GROUP

PALDAO AND QUILTED MAPLE

No. 3950 Chair
No. 3910 Dressers

For bedroom Pull-up Chairs see pages 40, 41, 42, 43
For Easy Chairs for the bedroom see pages 35, 36, 37, 38, 39

No. 3910 Bedside Table
D 14 W 16½ H 25

No. 3910 Dresser Base
W 48 D 18 H 33

No. 3910 Dresser Mirror
P 32 x 30

No. 3910 Bed
4 ft. 6 in. and 3 ft. 3 in
Headboard Height 33

The character of the following two bedroom groups is entirely different from Gilbert Rohde's previous work. His name has been associated with a rather severe but entirely functional style, but these groups are rich in decorative qualities and feeling of luxury. Mr. Rohde shows himself to be master of this style as he has been of functional design. Each of the suites combines many materials and uses both the curved and the straight line, but there is none of that confusion and disorganization of elements found so often when an attempt at luxury is made.

No. 3957 Vanity Chair
W 19 D 24 H $25\frac{1}{4}$
$1\frac{1}{3}$ Yards 50 in. Material

No. 3910 Vanity
No. 3957 Vanity Chair

In the No. 3910 group shown on these pages, the drawer fronts are slightly convex and covered in a newly perfected artificial leather in subtle tones of off-white and beige. The pulls for this suite are in the form of delicately thin strips of brushed brass.

The feature of this suite is the use of transparent legs. These are made of tubes of Lucite, which is a new colorless plastic. These legs have caps, also of brushed brass. A feeling of lightness, almost as if the pieces were suspended in air, is the effect obtained with this design.

No. 3910 Vanity Base
W 54 D $19\frac{1}{2}$ H 27

No. 3910 Vanity Mirror
P 26 x 26

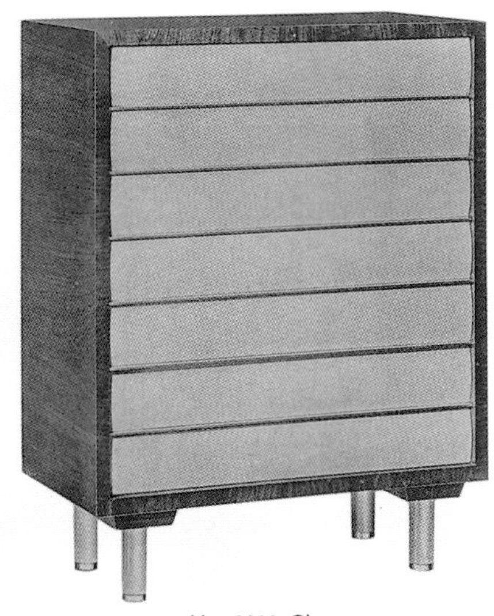

No. 3910 Chest
W 33 D 18 H $42\frac{1}{2}$

No. 3920 BEDROOM GROUP

EAST INDIA ROSEWOOD
AND
SEQUOIA BURL

No. 3920 Bed
No. 3920 Bedside Table
No. 3920 Vanity
No. 3951 Chair
No. 3943 Table
No. 3954 Bench

For bedroom Pull-up Chairs see pages 40, 41, 42, 43
For Easy Chairs for the bedroom see pages 35, 36, 37, 38, 39

No. 3920 Bedside Table
W 15 D 12 H 25

No. 3920 Dresser Table
W 46 D 19½ H 33

No. 3920 Dresser Mirror
P 32 Dia.

No. 3920 Bed
4 ft. 6 in. and 3 ft. 3 in.

In the No. 3920 group, Mr. Rohde emphasizes the use of Plexiglas for the pulls, combined with brushed brass decorative elements. The Plexiglas used for the pulls is a crystal-clear plastic that catches highlights with the brilliance of a diamond.

The same new off-white and beige artificial leather is used to cover the head and foot of the bed and also on portions of the cases.

The vanity in this suite as well as the No. 3910 is unique; this one in having adjustable circular triplex mirrors, framed in delicately thin brushed brass frames.

No. 3968 Chair
No. 3920 Dressers

No. 3920 Chest
W 34 D 19½ H 44¼

No. 3954 Bench
W 19 D 21¾ H 20
5/6 Yd. 50-in. Material

No. 3951 Easy Chair
W 29 D 37½ H 30
Seat Height 16
3 Yds. 50-in. Material

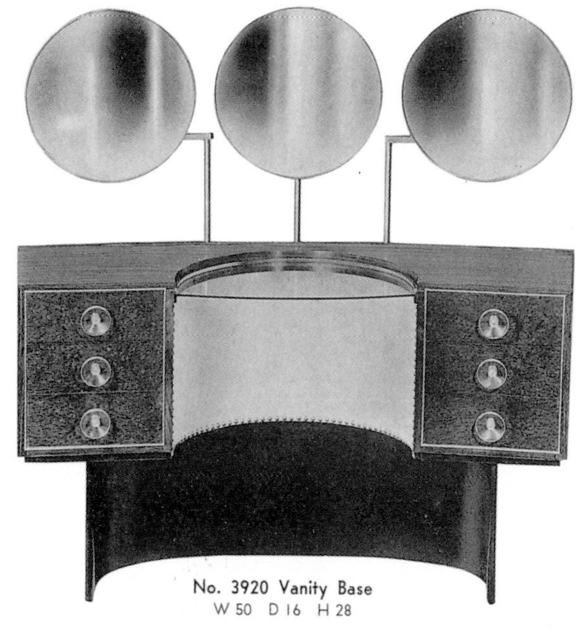

No. 3920 Vanity Base
W 50 D 16 H 28

No. 3920 Vanity Mirror
P 15 Dia.

No. 4010
BEDROOM GROUP
WALNUT AND AMERICAN ASH

The standard finish for the Walnut tops and ends and headend is usually Miller Grey and the Ash fronts and footend laid in parquetry fashion in a honey color. This combination of colors and of a fine and a coarse grained wood is unique and pleasing. The exaggerated saucer shaped pulls of dark wood with bright brass centers are arranged like the buttons on a cadet uniform. Also note the streamlined supports.

No. 4010 Vanity
L 54 D 20 H 26½
Mirror 30 x 32

No. 4010 Bedside Table
L 15 D 12½ H 25

No. 4010 Bed
4' 6" or 3' 3"
Headboard Height 32
Footboard Height 20½

No. 4010 BEDROOM GROUP

WALNUT AND AMERICAN ASH

Designed by Gilbert Rohde

No. 4030 Chair
W 25 D 31 H 29½
Seat Height 17
4 Yards 50 in. Material
Airtex-rubber knife-edged Cushions

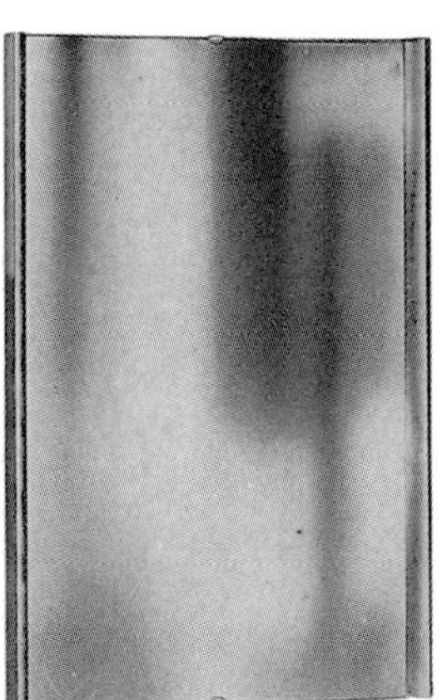

No. 4010 Dresser
L 48 D 19 H 32½
Mirror 33½ x 20

No. 4010 Chest
L 36 D 19 H 45½

This chair-tilt padded headboard makes reading in bed more comfortable. It is usually upholstered in a light brown imitation leather channelled with brass nails. Other colors, of course, are available.

The headend can be used with other footends in a line and is available in the 4' 6" and 3' 3" sizes and also in the 6' 5" width required with the Seng twin type frames described and illustrated on page 55.

No. 4012 Bed
4' 6" or 3' 3"
Headboard Height 32
Footboard Height 20½

No. 4014 Bed
Same Headboard as No. 4012 except
6' 5" long with Seng Twin Type Frames

No. 4080 BEDROOM GROUP

Designed by John Gartman

No. 4080 Chest
L 36 D 21 H 48

No. 4080 Dresser
L 54 D 18 H $32\frac{1}{2}$
Mirror 29 x 35

No. 4080 Chair
Overall Size 20 x 19 H 32
$\frac{3}{4}$ Yard 50 in. Material

No. 4080 Panel Bed
4' 6" and 3' 3"
Headboard Height 34
Footboard Height 21

No. 4080 BEDROOM GROUP

Designed by John Gartman

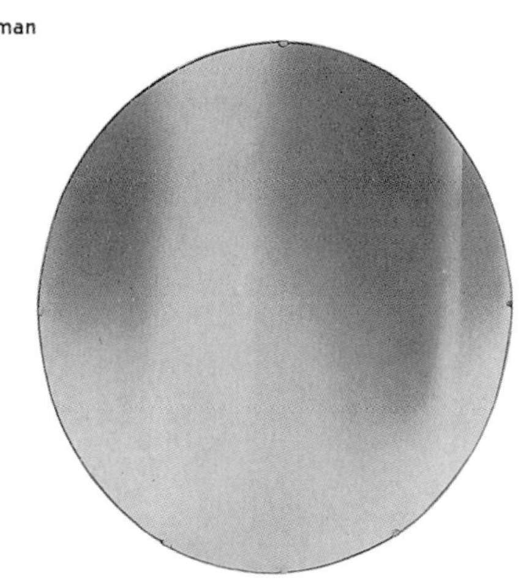

This group is available in either Paldao or Prima Vera.

The Prima Vera is usually furnished in a Harvest Mahogany color but can also be bleached to a very pale shade.

Paldao is a Philippine wood with easy moving grain. Finished in a dark Walnut color, considerable depth in the wood grain is revealed. Paldao can also be finished in a light grey color.

Pulls are of solid brass shaped like a violin string tightener. Mouldings painted gold to match the pulls.

No. 4080 Vanity
L 50 D 20 H 28
Mirror 32" dia.

No. 4082 Mirror Bed
4' 6" or 3' 3"

No. 4080 Ottoman
Overall Size 24 x 15 H 18
2 Yards

No. 4081 Bedside Table
T 16½ x 18 H 27½

No. 4081 Upholstered Bed
4' 6" or 3' 3"
Headboard Height 34
Footboard Height 10
½ Yard 54 in. Material
Tufted Headboard is Standard

TRADITIONAL GROUPS

THE Traditional line on the following pages has been planned to meet a real need. Time upon time the store or decorator is called upon to submit an ensemble of correlated pieces of authentic but uncommon design; matched in finish (sometimes in special finishes); of one high standard of quality; custom upholstered in harmonizing fabrics; not overpriced; preferably shipped at one time.

When such a need arises you will find it comparatively simple to plan your client's interior from these pages; and the selection and ordering from one source will greatly simplify your task.

Mahogany and Pine are used as harmonizing woods. Herman Miller Furniture Company has made pine furniture for a number of years. Pine pieces can be used altogether, or as complementing pieces with Mahogany. The two standard Mahogany finishes are Goddard and Museum. Goddard Mahogany is a hand-glazed, hand-padded finish, not distressed, and of substantial body. Museum is hand-distressed and hand-glazed, slightly lighter in color and body than Goddard. Both are block rubbed by hand.

The Pine finishes are Whittaker and Cambridge. Whittaker is a hand-treated finish not distressed, but giving the appearance of years of aging. Cambridge Pine is hand-distressed and antiqued to give the musty effect of a painted pine antique, washed off and restored.

Samples of the standard finishes sent on request. Special finishes can be matched for approximately 15% extra.

The same quality features in finish and upholstery and construction described on page 1 are found in the Traditional line.

LIVING ROOM

No. 735 Tuxedo Sofa
Overall size 74 x 30
Between Arms 65 H 32
Seat Height 19
9 Yards
Mahogany

No. 743 Open Arm Chair
Overall size 26 x 34
Between Arms 21 H 37
Seat Height 17 1¾ Yards
Mahogany

No. 756 Coffee Table
Top 32 x 17½ H 18
Pine

No. 6003 Table
L 13 W 13 H 31
Mahogany

No. 803 Breakfront Bookcase
W 64 D 17½ H 83
All Mahogany
Can also be used with 801 Dining Group on pages 76, 77
Desk Compartment in Top Drawer

No. 760 Coffee Table
T 32 x 16 H 21
Mahogany

LIVING ROOM

No. 742 Ladies' Club Chair
Overall size 31 x 30
Between Arms 21 H 36
Seat Height 19
5⅔ Yards
Mahogany

No. 3407 Desk
T 50 x 22 H 30
Pine
Leather Top

No. 600 Breakfront Bookcase
Base 56 x 17 H 81
Pine or Mahogany
Leather covered Writing Lid in top upper drawer

No. 604 Mirror
P 30 x 16
Pine

No. 3487 Low Chest
Top 31 x 18 H 31
Pine or Mahogany
Leather covered Writing Lid

LIVING ROOM

No. 600 Bookcase
T 17 x 56 H 81
Lacquered on Pine
Raised Chinese Decoration in Black, Red or Yellow.
Leather covered Writing Lid on top of upper drawer.

No. 749 Barrel Chair
Overall size 31 x 24
Between Arms 22 H 35
Seat Height 19
2½ Yards Inside
1⅓ Yards Outside
Mahogany

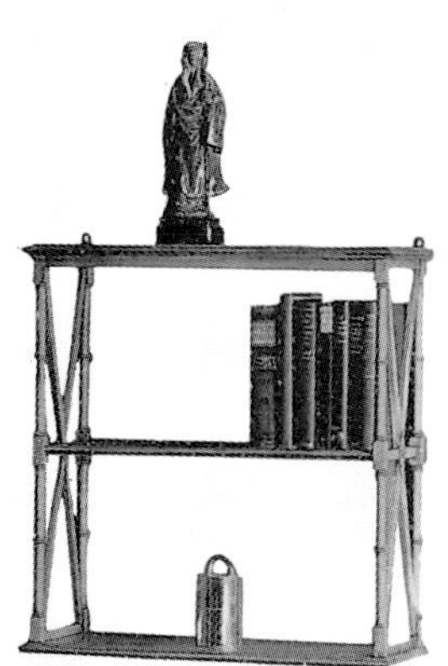

No. 762 Book Rack
W 22 D 8 H 22
Pine

No. 751 Table
No. 747 Sofa
No. 756 Coffee Table
No. 3506 Chair
No. 754 Table
No. 759 Bookshelf
No. 737 Chair

LIVING ROOM

No. 717 Desk
B $27\frac{1}{2}$ x 54
H 30
Mahogany
Genuine Leather Top

No. 731 Barrel Chair
Overall size 33 x 27
Between Arms 21 H 37
Seat Height 17
$4\frac{3}{4}$ Yards
Birch

No. 702 Arm Chair
W 24 D 23 H 36
$1\frac{1}{2}$ yards 50-in. material
Birch

No. 717 Desk
B $27\frac{1}{2}$ x 54
H 30
Mahogany

No. 3488 Bookcase
T 36 x $12\frac{1}{2}$ H 72
Pine Only
Plain Back

LIVING ROOM

No. 3513 Desk
L 40 W 19
Pine and Mahogany
Leather Top

No. 3387 Console Mirror
P 16 x 30
Finishes:
Decoration D — As Shown — Old Blue
Decoration S — Simpler — Off White
Old Plymouth Maple

No. 740 Chippendale Occasional Chair
Overall size 31 x 25
Between Arms 22 H 36
Seat Height 17
3 Yards
Mahogany

No. 740 Chair
No. 755 Table
No. 758 Coffee Table
No. 732 Sofa
No. 748 Chair

LIVING ROOM

No. 3416 Corner Cabinet
Pine Only
B 29 x 11 H 70

No. 734 Love Seat
Overall size 61 x 31
Between Arms 45 H 34
Seat Height 18
$6\frac{1}{2}$ Yards Mahogany

No. 738 Lounge Chair
Overall size 32 x 27
Between Arms 22 H 36
Seat Height 20
$4\frac{2}{3}$ Yards
Mahogany

No. 739 Tuxedo Chair
Overall size 34 x 32
Between Arms 21 H 33
Seat Height 18
$4\frac{2}{3}$ Yards
Mahogany

No. 3415 Corner Cabinet
Pine Only
B 29 x 11 H 70

LIVING ROOM

No. 737 Occasional Chair
Overall size 32 x 28
Between Arms 22 H 38
Seat Height 18
3⅔ Yards
Mahogany

No. 754 Living-Dining Table
L 54 W 23 H 31
All Mahogany

No. 751 Double Tier Table
L 30 W 17½ H 27
All Mahogany

No. 759 Bookshelf
W 29 D 10 H 37
All Mahogany

No. 747 Sofa
Overall Size 74 x 34
Between Arms 65 H 34
Seat Height 18
10 Yards
Mahogany
Specify Button or Plain Back

No. 709 Dresser Mirror
30 x 24
Pine Bamboo

LIVING ROOM

No. 612 Desk
L 50 W 24 H 30
Genuine Leather Top
Mahogany and Birch

No. 700 Chair
W 19 D 19 H 32
1 Yard 50-in. Material
Birch
This chair with diamond tufted
Seat and Back is No. 777

No. 761 Round 2 Tier Table
20 in. Diam. H 26
Goddard Mahogany

No. 709 Vanity Mirror
34 x 28
Pine Bamboo

No. 746 Love Seat
No. 3506 Chair

LIVING ROOM

No. 746 Duncan Phyfe Love Seat
Overall size 49 x 21
Between Arms 45½ H 34
Seat Height 17
2¼ Yards
Mahogany

No. 3507 Arm Chair
W 22½ D 20 H 37
¾ Yd. 50-in. Material
Birch

No. 3506 Chair
W 20 D 19 H 37
⅔ Yard 50-in. Material
Birch

No. 748 Open Arm Chair
Overall size 29 x 25
Between Arms 23 H 40
Seat Height 17
2⅓ Yards
Mahogany

No. 901 Breakfront Bookcase
W 54 D 16 H 77
Mahogany and Birch
Leather Covered Pull-out Lid

LIVING ROOM

No. 744 Wing Chair
Overall size 31 x 29
Between Arms 20 H 43
Seat Height 18
5½ Yards Mahogany

No. 807 Desk
L 44 D 22 H 30
Mahogany only
Leather Top

No. 758 Coffee Table
T 34 x 19 H 18
Pine or All Mahogany

No. 736 Open Arm Chair
Overall size 27 x 24
Between Arms 23 H 37
Seat Height 17
1⅔ Yards
Mahogany

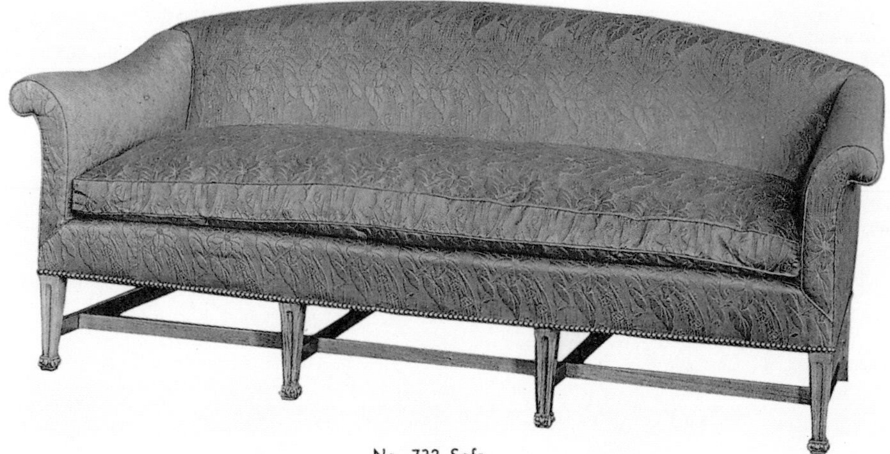

No. 732 Sofa
Overall size 82 x 33
Between Arms 66 H 32
Seat Height 19 8⅚ Yards
Birch

LIVING ROOM

No. 745 Hepplewhite Love Seat
Overall size 57 x 27
Between Arms 38 H 33
Seat Height 17
4½ Yards
Mahogany

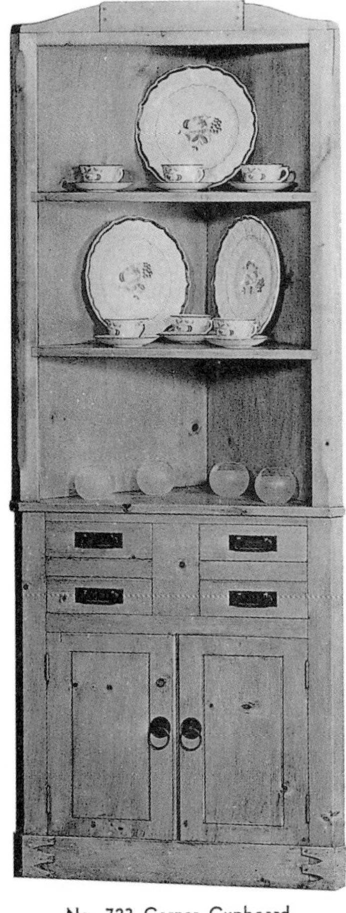

No. 723 Corner Cupboard
W 28 D 15 H 71½
Pine

No. 741 Occasional Chair
Channel Back
Overall size 32 x 28
Between Arms 21 H 38
Seat Height 18 4 Yards
Mahogany

No. 810 Desk
Rear
Note Mitre Corners giving an unusually trim effect

No. 810 Desk
L 49 D 25 H 30
Mahogany
Tooled Leather Top

REGENCY LIVING ROOM

ALL MAHOGANY

"Regency" is a term now applied to the decorative arts which overlaps the period when George, Prince of Wales, was Regent, and covers the work in the new classic style a decade before the institution of the Regency in 1811, and after the accession of George IV as King in 1820.

No. 421 Desk
L 54 D 30 H 30

No. 412 Lamp Table
L 16½ D 16½ H 28

Adapted from Mahogany Library Table of pedestal form. Circa 1800. From Messrs. F. Partridge.

Note the deep vertical filing drawer is placed at a convenient height.

No. 418 Coffee Table
L 30 D 19 H 19
Glass Top

No. 416 End Table
L 31 D 17 H 26

No. 411 End Table
L 27 D 16 H 25
Storage for phonograph record albums

No. 417 Double Bookcase
L 27 D 23½ H 47
Mahogany and Birch

REGENCY LIVING ROOM

ALL MAHOGANY

No. 414 Lamp Table
L 28 D 22 H 27

No. 413 Lamp Table
L 30 D 30 H 28

No. 419 Coffee Table
L 28 D 28 H 18
Glass Top

No. 410 Console Bookcase
L 44 D 13 H 38

Motive adapted from Rosewood Cupboard in The Mill Cottage, Burford, England. Note the space for phonograph record albums. Can also be furnished with grille doors.

FORMAL DINING ROOM

ALL MAHOGANY

No. 801 Buffet
L 68 D 22 H 36
All Mahogany

No. 802 Arm Chair
Overall size $23\frac{1}{2}$ x 19 H $39\frac{1}{2}$
Between Arms 20
$\frac{2}{3}$ Yard
All Mahogany

No. 801 Chair
Overall size $19\frac{1}{2}$ x $17\frac{1}{2}$ H $39\frac{1}{2}$
$\frac{2}{3}$ Yard
All Mahogany

No. 801 Server
L 31 D 17 H 32
All Mahogany

No. 801 China
W 40 D 16 H $75\frac{1}{2}$

No. 801 Table
Top Closed 66 x 44
Top Open 96 x 44
2 15-in. Fillers
All Mahogany

Also see No. 803 Breakfront, page 71, for a suitable piece with this group

FORMAL DINING ROOM

ALL MAHOGANY

No. 702 Arm Chair
W 24 D 23 H 36
1½ Yds. 50-in. Material
Birch

No. 803 Console Table
L 45 D 21 H 30
All Mahogany

No. 802 Table
Top Closed 45 x 26
Top Open 45 x 68
H 30
All Mahogany

No. 701 Side Chair
W 20½ D 23 H 36
1⅓ Yds. 50-in. Material
Birch

No. 401 REGENCY DINING ROOM

ALL MAHOGANY

No. 401 Table
Top Closed 56 x 38
Top Extended 86 x 38
H 30

No. 401 China
W 31 D 17 H 78

Adapted from Mahogany Secretaire Cabinet. Cornice surmounted by carved eagle and two flammate urns.

No. 401 Arm Chair
Overall Size 23 x 22½ H 34
Seat 20 x 17½
⅔ Yard 50 in. Material

Adapted from painted and gilt arm chair by George Smith. Circa 1810. From H. Goodhart Rendel, Esq. 13 Crawford Street.

REGENCY DINING ROOM

No. 401 Buffet
L 54 D 22 H 36

Adapted from Mahogany Breakfront Sideboard, inlaid with Satinwood panels. Circa 1800. From Messrs. Botibol.

No. 402 Side Chair
Overall Size 22 x 19 H 33
Seat 16 x 13½
⅔ Yard 50 in. Material

Adapted from Chair — Circa 1810. From Edward Hudson, Esq.

No. 402 Credenza
L 54 D 22 H 36

Original Mahogany Pedestal Sideboard. Circa 1810. From Sir John Hall. We have made it into a junior credenza in order to give added storage space.

No. 711 BEDROOM GROUP

ALL MAHOGANY

No. 711 Chest
B 38 x 21 H 50
All Mahogany

BEDSIDE TABLE, MIRROR FRAMES AND VANITY USUALLY IN PINE

No. 711 Bedside Table
T 17 x 13 H 28
All Mahogany or Pine

No. 711 Bench
T 23 x 16 H 22
Seat Height 18
5/6 Yd. 50-in. Material
Birch finished Pine or Mahogany

No. 711 Bed
W 4 ft. 6 in. or 3 ft. 3 in.
All Mahogany

No. 738 Lounge Chair
Overall size 32 x 27
Between Arms 22 H 36
Seat Height 20
4 2/3 Yards
Mahogany

No. 711 BEDROOM GROUP

ALL MAHOGANY

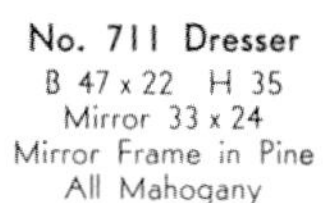

No. 711 Vanity
B 48 x 22 H 30
Mirror 28 x 23
Mirror Frame in Pine
All Mahogany or Pine

No. 711 Dresser
B 47 x 22 H 35
Mirror 33 x 24
Mirror Frame in Pine
All Mahogany

No. 711 Chair
Overall size 18 x 16 H 33
Seat Height 18
3/4 Yd. 50-in. Material
Birch finished Mahogany or Pine

No. 712 Bed
W 4 ft. 6 in. or 3 ft. 3 in.
All Mahogany

No. 403 REGENCY BEDROOM GROUP

ALL MAHOGANY

GODDARD FINISH

No. 403 Dresser
L 48 D 22 H 36
Mirror 24 x 40

No. 403 Bedside Table
W 14 D 16 H 29½

The rope or twist mouldings on corner of case pieces and the key designs on the fronts are motifs adapted for Regency pieces.

No. 403 Bed
4' 6" or 3' 3"
Headboard Height 45
Footboard Height 24½

REGENCY BEDROOM GROUP

No. 403 Chest
W 37 D 20 H 48

No. 402 Chair
Overall Size 22 x 19 H 33
Seat 16 x 13½
⅔ Yard 50 in. Material

No. 403 Bench
Overall Size 26 x 15 H 21
Seat 23 x 13
½ Yard

No. 403 Vanity
L 49 D 19 H 33
Mirror 22 x 30

No. 805 BEDROOM GROUP

ALL MAHOGANY
HOLLY INLAY

No. 805 Chair
Seat 18 x 17 H 17
Overall Height 32
1/2 Yard

No. 805 Chest
T 34 x 19 H 49

Ample storage space behind the smooth working tambour doors.

No. 805 Bedside Table
T 16 1/2 x 14 H 27 1/2

No. 805 Bed
Width 4 ft. 6 in. or 3 ft. 3 in.

No. 805 BEDROOM GROUP

ALL MAHOGANY

HOLLY INLAY

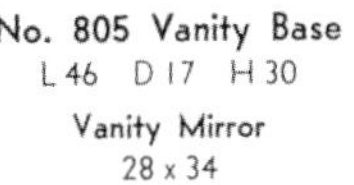

No. 805 Vanity Base
L 46 D 17 H 30

Vanity Mirror
28 x 34

No. 805 Bench
Seat 23 x 16 H 17
2/3 Yard

No. 805 Dresser Base
L 45 D 20 H 35½

Dresser Mirror
28 x 32

SHAKER FURNITURE

The following are adaptations from the craft details and ideals of Shaker furniture.

The Shakers, as you no doubt know, were an American communal sect who believed that ornamentation was sin. Thus they practiced the functionalism and simplicity which Modern designers are seeking to achieve.

These pieces are in Knotty Pine finished in either our Whittaker or Cambridge finishes.

No. 723 China
W 30 D 15 H 62
Pine

No. 784 Flat Top Desk
B 50 x 22 H 30
Pine

No. 780 Smoker Table
T 28 x 16 H 24
Pine

No. 721 Desk
B 46 x 20 H 31
Mirror 24 x 32

No. 785 Living-Dining Table
Top Closed 60 x 20
Top Open 60 x 40
Height 30
Pine

LAMPS

This page illustrates a group of Modern lamps by prominent present-day designers.

Note from the price list that in quantities of less than six lamps there is a packaging charge to be added.

Drop shipments are made from New York City.

No. 41133 Table Lamp
Base of spun aluminum. Two-light fixture. Height overall 19 in.; diameter of bottom of shade 22 in.; depth of shade 12 in. Shade of turquoise blue crash material over parchment, with silver strand trim.

No. 439 Table Lamp
Glazed green pottery with walnut. Height overall 19 in. Shade of natural shantung material over parchment, brown tuft trim at top.

No. 41126 Table Lamp
Base of brass with maple ring. Two light fixture. Height overall 22 in. — shade of white crash material over parchment.

No. 41125 — Aluminum and Walnut.

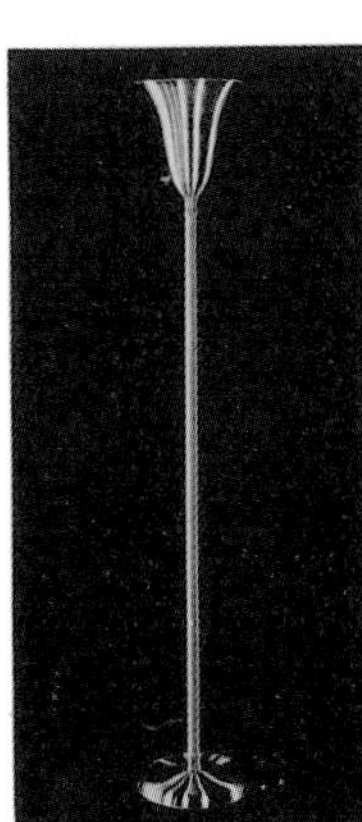

No. 41102 Torchiere
Bronze. Height of lamp 64½ in.; top diameter of shade 11 in. Three-way Mogul socket.

No. 4200 — Aluminum and Brass.

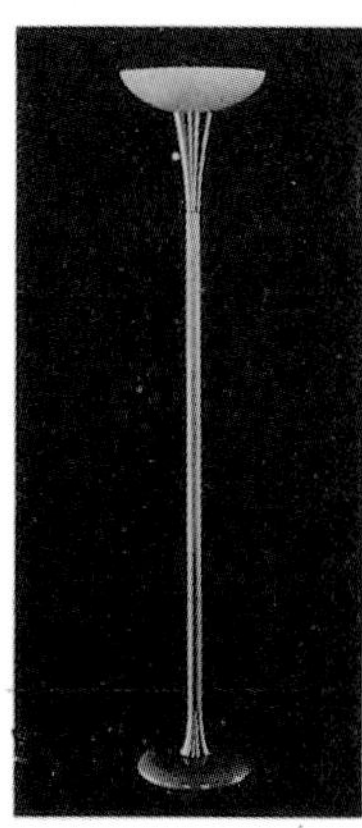

No. 4225 Torchiere
Aluminum, oak and glass shade. Three-way Mogul socket. Height 64 in. — diameter of glass shade 14 in.

No. 4224 — Maple and Brass.

No. 4216 — Walnut and Aluminum.

No. 4426 Table Lamp
Base and shade of natural reed. Height overall 16 in. Shade diameter 14 in. Baked white enamel eyeplate.

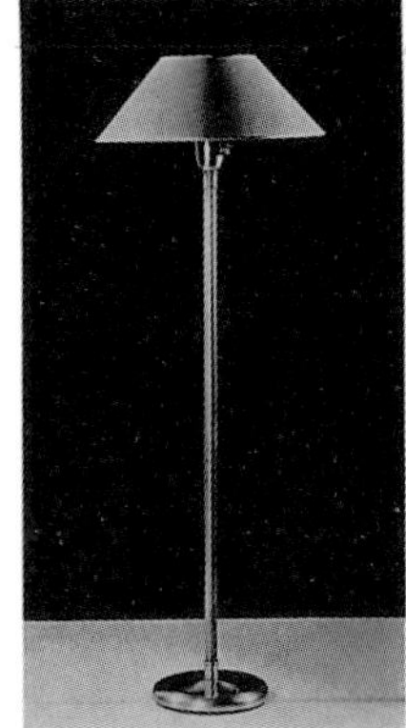

No. 41107 Floor Lamp
Bronze base. Height of lamp 57 in.; shade diameter 21 in. Shade of tan poplin over parchment, brass trim top and bottom.

No. 4215 Table Lamp (41139 Shade)
Twisted oak base. Two-light fixture. Height of lamp overall 21¾ in. Shade of eggshell tree bark fabric over parchment. Top diameter of shade 7¾ in.; bottom diameter 18½ in.; depth of shade 9¾ in.

No. 4223 Floor Lamp (41105 Shade)
Oak and aluminum base. Height of lamp 57 in.; shade diameter 20½ in. Shade of grey satin over parchment, with silver trim top and bottom.

No. 41132 Table Lamp
Brown alumilite base with maple ornament. Height overall 20½ in.; bottom diameter of shade 14 in.; depth of shade 9½ in. Shade of eggshell material toned with brown over parchment, with coarse brown trim top and bottom.

No. 41151 Vanity Lamp
Brass and chartreuse leather. Height of lamp 16 in. One light fixture. Shade diameter 6½ in. Shade of gold metallic paper and chartreuse leather.

No. 41121 — Brown Leather and Aluminum.

No. 41152 — White Leather and Bronze.

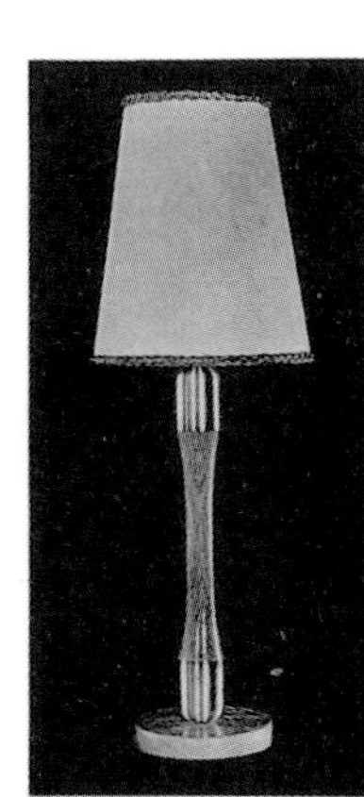

No. 41111 Vanity Lamp
Oak and brass; one light fixture. Eggshell shantung material shade with gold trim. Height of lamp overall 20½ in.; bottom diameter of shade 7¼ in.; top diameter of shade 4¾ in.; depth of shade 8¼ in.

No. 41140 Bridge Lamp
Oak column with brass arm and socket housing. Base of oak, trimmed with brass. One light. Height overall 55¼ in.; length of brass arm 16 in. Shade of tan coarse material over parchment — no trim. Diameter of shade 15½ in.; depth of shade 8½ in.

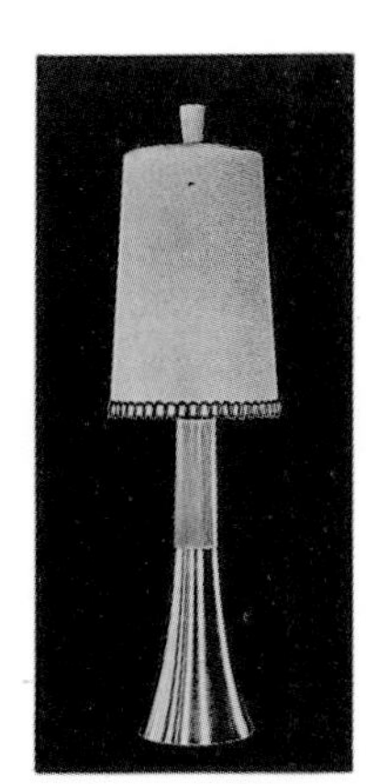

No. 41119 Vanity Lamp
Base of oak column on spun brass. One light fixture. Height overall 18¾ in.; top diameter of shade 4½ in.; bottom diameter 5¾ in.; depth of shade 8⅜ in. Shade of eggshell ribbed satin-like material, with gold and brown trim.

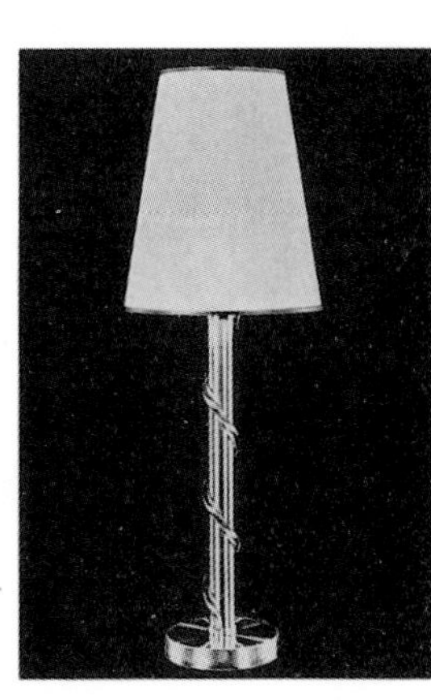

No. 41108 Vanity Lamp
Brass and Lucite. Height of lamp 19 in.; Shade diameter 8 in. One light fixture. Shade of white clair de lune, brass trim top and bottom.

NUMERICAL INDEX

SECTIONAL INDEX

The Herman Miller Catalog Supplement

Please add this Supplement to your Fall 1940 Catalog

THE HERMAN MILLER FURNITURE COMPANY

ZEELAND • MICHIGAN

Permanent Show Rooms for the Trade

One Park Ave., New York, N. Y. • J. M. Eppinga in Charge
1680 Merchandise Mart, Chicago • Tom Potter in Charge

PALDAO GROUP

The design of this group is extremely dignified and simple, yet luxurious, and will fit into any home. The tops and sides are Paldao; the burl fronts are Acacia.

The photograph at the left shows the group in a dark brown finish known as "Mink." The pieces are also available in a dark reddish brown called "Sable"; a light natural called "Beaver"; and a very light grey finish called "Persian Grey."

No. 4103 Utility Cabinet **No. 4102-G Bookcase**

No. 4101 Chest-Desk

Three grouping units from living-dining group made in Paldao and Acacia Burl. The large pulls are especially designed for this group and are finished in antique brass.

No. 4101 Chest-Desk (Open)
40 x 17" H 42"

Note place for typewriter.
This piece combines with pieces of the same size on pages 2 and 3.

No. 4101 Chest-Desk (Closed)
40 x 17" H 42"

Designed by G. Rohde

PALDAO GROUP

Tops and sides of Paldao (a Philippine wood with rather pronounced light and dark grain): fronts, Acacia Burl.

No. 4103 Utility Cabinet
40 x 17" H 42"

No. 4102-G Bookcase
40 x 17" H 42"

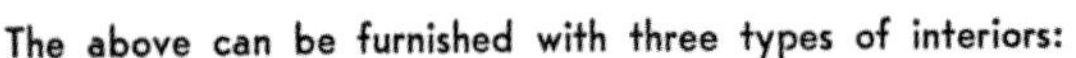

The above can be furnished with three types of interiors:

A — Two adjustable shelves across the entire width.
B — Two adjustable shelves in half the interior and the other half a unit consisting of five trays.
C — With two tray units of five trays each.

Be sure to specify the interior desired.

Besides this the No. 4103 is equipped with a radio interior as shown on page 3.

No. 4102-M Bookcase
40 x 17" H 42"

No. 4102-L Bookcase
40 x 17" H 42"

This can be supplied with a variety of doors

Without doors it is known as No. 4102.
With wood doors — No. 4102W.
With sliding glass doors — No. 4102G.
Leather-covered doors — No. 4102L.
Metal grille doors — No. 4102M.

The interiors are always dark but the exterior can be supplied in the following finishes described on page 1: Sable, Mink, Beaver, and Persian Grey.

These pieces combine with pieces of the same sizes shown on pages 1 and 3.

Footnote: — Corner pedestals can be supplied as fillers where an L-shaped corner grouping is required of the cabinets shown on pages 1, 2, and 3:

No. 41110 Corner Filler 17 x 17" top, 42" high
No. 41111 Corner Filler 13 x 17" top, 42" high
No. 41112 Corner Filler 13 x 13" top, 42" high

Designed by G. Rohde

PALDAO GROUP

For description of woods, finishes, choice of doors, and combinations, see pages 1 and 2.

No. 4113 Bookcase
21¼ x 13" H 42"

This lines up with No. 4112.

For a bookcase of the same length and height but 17" deep to line up with No. 4102, order No. 4114.

No. 4113 and No. 4114 can be fitted with one door, either wood, leather, metal grille, or cane. No glass door available.

No. 4112 Bookcase
40 x 13" H 42"

Same height and length as No. 4102 but only 13" deep instead of 17". Can be equipped with the same doors as No. 4102.

No. 4103 Radio; No. 4114 Bookcase; large chair is No. 3950; Lamp Table No. 4187; Occasional Table No. 4186; Arm Chair No. 4196.

Tops and sides of cabinet are made of Paldao and the front of Acacia Burl. The pulls especially designed for this group are finished in antique brass.

The Cabinet can be furnished with or without equipment. Our standard equipment is the Wilcox-Gay Radio; phonograph with automatic record-changer and voice recorder.

No. 4103 Radio
40 x 17" H 42"

No. 4114 Bookcase
21¼ x 17" H 42"

No. 3950 Chair
W 38" D 37" H 29"
Seat Ht. 16"
5 Yards

No. 4196 Arm Chair
W 24" D 24" H 32"

Designed by G. Rohde

PALDAO GROUP

No. 4105 Breakfront
66 x 15" H 72"

No. 4165 Arm Chair
W 23" D 23" H 33"
$1\frac{1}{3}$ Yards

One of a large group of living-dining room pieces. The design is dignified and simple, yet luxurious.
The lower portion of the cabinet has four doors with slightly concave fronts.
The desk is in the upper unit.
The imposing pulls especially designed for this group are finished in antique brass.
The tops and sides and door fronts are made of Paldao.
The drop lid desk front is made of Acacia Burl.

No. 4100 Bookcase-Desk
60 x 17" H $49\frac{1}{2}$"

No. 3956 Chair
W 26" D 26" H 30"
2 Yards

A large, important unit that can be used as the focal unit in a room.

The tops and sides are of Paldao and the front and desk unit in center which is slightly concave is of Acacia Burl.

Footnote. The piece is available in four finishes: Mink, Sable, Beaver, and Persian Grey. The interiors are always dark.

Designed by G. Rohde

PALDAO LIVING ROOM GROUP

Low Cabinets and Bookshelves

Paldao tops and sides; wood doors, Acacia Burl.

Finishes: Mink, Sable, Beaver, and Persian Grey as described on page 1.

Doors available for No. 4107 and No. 4108 Low Cabinets are wood of Acacia Burl, cane, metal grille, sliding glass.

The cane and wood doors are as illustrated; the glass and metal grille are like those illustrated on page 2.

No. 4107 Low Cabinet
36 x 13" H 25"

No. 4108 Bookcase
36 x 13" H 25"

No. 4175 Chair
W 30" D 38" H 31"
6 Yards

No. 4186 Coffee Table
41 x 26½" H 15"

No. 4109 Low Utility Bookcase
65 x 13" H 25"

No. 4110 Bookshelves
54 x 15" H 29"

Designed by G. Rohde

PALDAO DESKS

Belong to a complete group of living room pieces in Paldao

No. 4115 Desk
56 x 28¾" H 29"

No. 3967-B Chair
W 24½" D 24¼" H 3
1½ Yards

No. 3956 Chair
W 26" D 26" H 30"
2 Yards

A shelf pulls out of one pedestal at the proper height for typewriter.

The top of this piece is kidney-shaped and the lines are everywhere soft and round. It is simple, yet luxurious, and will fit into any home and even combine with period pieces.

The sides of the pedestal are covered with leather cloth which is available in several colors to harmonize with the finishes.

The pulls are especially designed for this group and are finished in antique brass.

No. 4106 Desk
52 x 27" H 29"

No. 4164 Side Chair
W 20" D 23" H 33"
1⅓ Yards

No. 3965 Arm Chair
W 24" D 22" H 31"
2 Yards

No. 4106 Desk

Single pedestal, ectoplastic Desk

An unusual Modern version of a single pedestal flat top desk. The top is of an ectoplastic shape with constantly varying curves and straight lines.

Leather cloth is used on the sides of the pedestal and leg, available in different colors to match the different finishes.

Designed by G. Rohde

Footnote:— Finishes on the above desks: Mink, Sable, Beaver, and Persian Grey.

PALDAO GROUP

The pieces shown on this and the next three pages have been especially designed for the one and two-room apartments and living-dining rooms.

The No. 4160 Compact illustrated on this and the next page is a four-purpose furniture unit; Bookcase, Desk, China Cabinet, and Dining Unit.

The photograph at the left shows the closed view in which it appears to be a simple breakfront. The center cabinet in the lower portion of the unit houses a drop leaf dining table large, enough to seat six people. Above this is a desk. In the cabinet is a pigeon-hole unit for stationery and shelves for books and china. The small drawers in the side of the lower portion are for silverware.

The lower portion of the cabinet is made of Paldao available in four finishes: Mink, Sable, Beaver, and Persian Grey, as described on page 1. The upper portion is covered in a leather-like fabric decorated with gold stripes. Several leather colors are available to match the different finishes. The large pulls on the lower portion, especially designed for this piece, are in antique brass.

This piece is also available without the drop leaf table.

No. 4160 Compact
52 x 15" H 80"

No. 3665 Chair
W 18" D 21" H 31"
1 Yard

No. 3683 Chair
Overall 28¼ x 28¼" H 27"
Between Arms 22"
3¾ Yards

This view shows the unit in use as a desk. Note the pigeon-hole for stationery and shelves in the upper portion of the cabinet.

No. 3665 Chair **No. 4160 Compact** **No. 3683 Chair**

Designed by G. Rohde

PALDAO GROUP

This shows the unit with the lower compartment open which houses a drop leaf folding table. If only two are to dine, the table need not be removed and the diners sit in close proximity to the cabinet within reach of the dishes. The table can be opened and closed in a second with only two motions.

No. 4160 Compact

No. 4160 Compact No. 3665 Chairs

This view shows the drop leaf folding table entirely removed and opened up large enough to serve six people.

No. 4160 Compact

No. 3665 Chairs

No. 3683 Chair

Designed by G. Rohde

PALDAO LIVING-DINING GROUP

No. 4104 Cabinet
66 x 15" H 33"

This shows two dinette utility chests, both of them equipped with silver and linen trays and shelf compartments.

Note that the doors are slightly concave.

The large pulls especially designed for this group are finished antique brass.

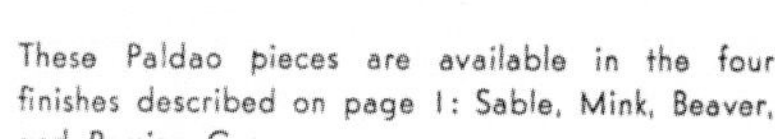

These Paldao pieces are available in the four finishes described on page 1: Sable, Mink, Beaver, and Persian Grey.

No. 4116 Dining Utility Chest
49½ x 15" H 33"

Designed by G. Rohde

PALDAO LIVING-DINING UNITS

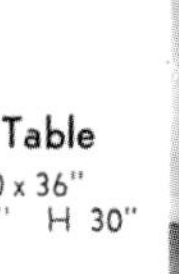

No. 4166 Table
Closed — 20 x 36"
Open — 36 x 76" H 30"

No. 3665 Chair
W 18" D 21" H 31"
1 Yard

No. 4165 Arm Chair
W 23" D 23" H 33"
1⅓ Yards

No. 4194 Hall Console
49 x 15" H 29"

No. 4166 Console Extension Table shown open and closed.

No. 4166 Extension Table
Closed — 20 x 36"
Open — 36 x 76" H 30"

No. 4117 Drop Leaf Gateleg
Closed — 36" x 12"
Open — 36 x 65½" H 29"

No. 4117 Drop Leaf Extension Table is shown partly open. This can be used as a console, a writing table, or a dining table seating six people.

Designed by G. Rohde

PALDAO TABLES

The tables shown on this and the next three pages belong to the large group of living-dining units illustrated on pages 1 to 10.

No. 4124 Game Table
32 x 32" H 29"

No. 4165 Arm Chair
W 23" D 23" H 33"
1⅓ Yards

No. 4164 Side Chair
W 20" D 23" H 33"
1⅓ Yards

A checkerboard is inlaid in the center of the top. The table contains two drawers for cards or chessmen. At the corners are metal cups sunk into the surface, which ordinarily serve as ash trays, but when the wire grids are left off the cups serve as glass-holders.

The legs are covered in a leather fabric which is available in several colors to match the different finishes of the table.

The bentwood chairs shown here are a new and graceful design in this style of unbreakable small chair.

In the background is shown a long low chest with four concave doors, No. 4104.

The sides of the Game Table are also slightly concave.

No. 4168 Nest of Tables
26 x 16¼" H 27"
21 x 14½" H 25"
17¼ x 12¾" H 23"

No. 4169 Serving Cart
34 x 17" H 32"

Top tray is glass; second and third trays, cork.

The handle and the lower side panels are covered in leather cloth. A tambour door makes the lower compartment very accessible.

Finishes: Mink, Sable, Beaver, and Persian Grey.

No. 4183 Corner Table
32 x 32" H 21½"

This is a table which is primarily useful to take the place of a corner chair in a combination chair arrangement. It also serves as a sofa end table or a coffee table.

Designed by G. Rohde

Group of glass and wood top tables with leather legs and nail trim. The nail trim is regularly put on the outside.

No. 4178 Sofa
W 78" D 32" H 29"
66" between arms
11 Yards

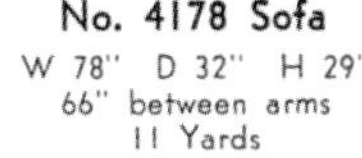

No. 4126 Table
44 x 22" H 15½"

No. 4127 Glass Top Table
34" Dia. H 15½"

No. 4189 Fireside Table
48 x 18" H 16"

No. 4125 Coffee Table
44 x 22" H 15"

No. 4128 Glass Top Table
28" Dia. H 15½"

Designed by G. Rohde

PALDAO TABLES

At the left is the answer to the demand for bigger and better Coffee Tables. For a room that can take it, what would be more imposing than such a table and how useful it would be.

Numbers 4187 and 4186 are first cousins in a Lamp and Coffee Table, unconventional in shape but very dignified and luxurious. The leather-cloth covered legs usually have the nail trim on the outside. Another view of No. 4186 is shown on page 5.

Woods used: Paldao edges; Acacia Burl tops. Available in the four standard finishes: Mink, Sable, Beaver, and Persian Grey.

No. 4186 Coffee Table
41 x 26½" H 15"

No. 4188 Coffee Table
44 x 44" H 15"

No. 4187 Lamp Table
27 x 22" H 27"

No. 4129 End Table
28 x 16" H 22"

No. 4122 Lamp Table to match
28 x 16" H 27"

No. 4123 Lamp Table
24" Dia. H 27"

Designed by G. Rohde

PALDAO GROUP TABLES

Conventional shapes and sizes. Leather cloth legs with nail trim always on the outside unless otherwise specified.

Acacia Burl tops.

Available in the usual finishes: Mink, Sable, Beaver, Persian Grey.

No. 4118 Coffee Table
36 x 18" H 17"

No. 4121 Coffee Table
36" Dia. H 15"

No. 4120 Coffee Table
30" Dia. H 17"

No. 4119 Coffee Table
44 x 22" H 15"

Designed by G. Rohde

MODERN SEATING PIECES

The next four pages illustrate the upholstered units that have been added to the already large line shown in the current catalogue.

The No. 4176 and No. 4175 pieces appear low; yet the seats are so luxuriously soft that the sitter sinks down enough so that the back cushion serves as a head rest. A profile view of the No. 4175 chair is shown on page 5.

No. 4176 Sofa
W 73" D 38" H 31"
66" between arms
11 Yards

No. 4170 Chair
W 25" D 27½" H 33"
4½ Yards
An all around chair for home and office use.

No. 4172 Chair
W 26" D 26" H 30"
4 Yards

No. 4175 Chair
W 30" D 38" H 31"
6 Yards

Designed by G. Rohde

[16]

No. 4178 Sofa
W 78" D 32" H 29"
66" between arms
11 Yards

No. 4126 Glass Top Table
44 x 22" H 15½"

No. 4177 Chair
W 34" D 32" H 29"
6 Yards

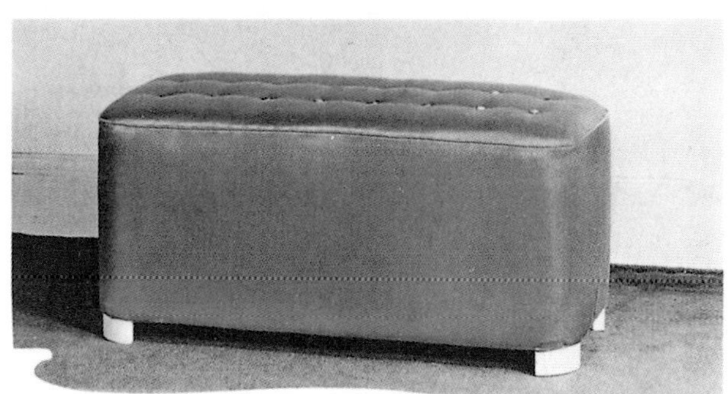

No. 4199 Footend Bench
36 x 15" H 16"
1⅔ Yards

A comfortable bench that is especially designed for placing at the foot of a bed. It will tie in with any of the Modern bedroom groups.

No. 4140 Vanity Chair
W 21" D 22" H 25"
2 Yards

No. 4141 Vanity Bench
W 19" D 19½" H 22½"
1 Yard

Designed by G. Rohde

No. 4162 Side Chair
W 20" D 22" H 31"
5/6 Yard

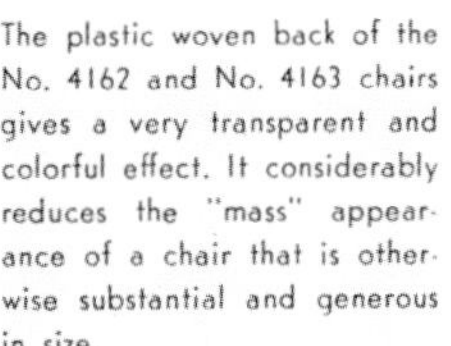

The plastic woven back of the No. 4162 and No. 4163 chairs gives a very transparent and colorful effect. It considerably reduces the "mass" appearance of a chair that is otherwise substantial and generous in size.

No. 4163 Arm Chair
W 24" D 22" H 31"
5/6 Yard

No. 4196 Arm Chair
W 24" D 24" H 32"
1 1/2 Yards

No. 4195 Side Chair
W 22" D 24" H 32"
1 1/2 Yards

No. 4164 Side Chair
W 20" D 23" H 33"
1 1/3 Yards

No. 4165 Arm Chair
W 23" D 23" H 33"
1 1/3 Yards

The interior at the right is primarily shown here for the sake of illustrating the No. 4164 and No. 4165 bentwood chairs. This is a bentwood design light in appearance but practically unbreakable.

Designed by G. Rohde

This illustrates an innovation in chair design. You can tell it came from an architect's drafting room; the side supports like a compass and the seats like a protractor. The result is a lightweight chair of very substantial construction. Its use is not limited to the home. It has great possibilities in institutions and stores.

No. 4171 Chair
W 20½" D 21" H 27½"
¾ Yards

Designed by Allan Gould

PALDAO DINING ROOM GROUP WITH TWO TYPES OF TABLES

No. 4190 Buffet

No. 4190 Table
68 x 40" 96" Extended

No. 4196 Arm Chair

No. 4195 Side Chair

No. 4190 Buffet (Closed)
72 x 19" 34" High

Perhaps the first table that ever frankly invited your guests to rest their feet under your table. The leather cloth will stand worlds of scuffing and when finally it does begin to show unsightly wear, the base is very easv to recover. Note the inlay in the top.

No. 4190 Buffet (Open)
72 x 19" 34" High

The No. 4190 Buffet shown open and closed has velvet-lined trays for silverware, cork-lined trays for glassware, and linen trays. The Buffet has four pullout boards of unique design. They are made of unfinished Oak, the two at the end being suitable for cutting boards and the center one for use as a cheese and meat board. These features make this particularly serviceable for buffet suppers.

The base is leather cloth covered and brass nail trim. The large pulls were especially designed for this group and are finished in antique brass.

The Dinette Utility Chests shown on page 9 could also be used with this group.

Designed by G. Rohde

The octagon legs are covered with leather cloth and brass nail trim on the outside..

4192 Table is a round top table 50" diameter which extends to 98" Same type of leather cloth legs as No. 4191.

No. 4191 Table
68 x 40" 96" Extended

No. 4192 Table
50" Dia. 98" Extended

No. 4190 China
33 x 14" 70" High

No. 4190 Server
33 x 14" 29½" High

The China has two sliding glass doors. The China back is in lemon gold. The base of this China can be used as a Server. Call it No. 4190 Server.

No. 4196 Arm Chair
W 24" D 24" H 32"
1½ Yards

No. 4194 Server
49 x 15" 29" High

Leather cloth legs with nail trim. This can also be used as a Hall Console.

The No. 4194 and No. 4195 Chairs while designed specially for this suite, can be used with other groups and in turn other dining chairs shown in the catalogue can be used with this dining group. Made in Birch.

No. 4195 Side Chair
W 22" D 24" H 32"
1½ Yards

Paldao veneer finished in the four standard colors: Mink, Sable, Beaver, and Persian Grey.

Designed by G. Rohde

No. 4130 BEDROOM GROUP

White Oak finished in two very lovely colors: Antelope, a light finish; Silver Fox, very dark, with leather pulls and feet to match. Bed also carries the same leather trim as on the pulls.

No. 4130 Dresser Base
46 x 18½" H 33"

No. 4130 Dresser Mirror
20 x 34"

No. 4130 Lingerette
19 x 18½" H 33"

The Dresser can be used in pairs or if there is not wall space enough available for Twin Dressers, a Dresser and Lingerette can be used together as an architectural unit.

No. 3323 Ottoman
Dia. 18" H 17"
1½ Yards

No. 4130 Bed
4' 6" or 3' 3" Head 35" Foot 21"

No. 4131 Bed 6' 6" with twin-type metal frames like our No. 3631 on page 55 of 1940 catalog.

No. 4130 Bedside Table
16 x 13" H 25"

Designed by G. Rohde

No. 4130 Chest

No. 4130 Vanity Base
49 x 18" H 27"

No. 4130 Vanity Mirror
24 x 30"

No. 3665 Chair
W 18" D 21" H 31"
1 Yard

No. 4130 Chest
33 x 15½" H 46"

Designed by G. Rohde

No. 4140 BEDROOM GROUP

Mahogany and leather cloth. The Mahogany is available in a dark Piano Mahogany color and a light Cafe Au Lait color. Offwhite leather cloth panels are used on the fronts in combination with dark Mahogany and a tan leather cloth in combination with the light Mahogany.

No. 4140 Dresser Base
44½ x 19" H 34½"

No. 4140 Dresser Mirror
20 x 34"

Please note that the bedside table has a square back instead of rounded back as shown in the photograph.

No. 4140 Bed
4' 6" or 3' 3" Head 35" Foot 22"

No. 4142 Bed
6' 5" Head 35"

No. 4140 Bedside Table
18 x 13" H 25"

Three types of beds are available:

The No. 4140 is the reclining chair type, leather cloth covered headend with a veneered footend.

The No. 4142 is the same type of headend 6' 5" wide equipped with 2 twin-type steel frames.

The No. 4141 is the plain veneered headend with a low footend.

No. 4141 Vanity Bench
19 x 19" H 22"

Designed by G. Rohde

No. 4140 BEDROOM GROUP

No. 4140 Vanity Base
56 x 19" H 30"

No. 4140 Vanity Mirror
28 x 28"

No. 4140 Chest
34½ x 19" H 44½"

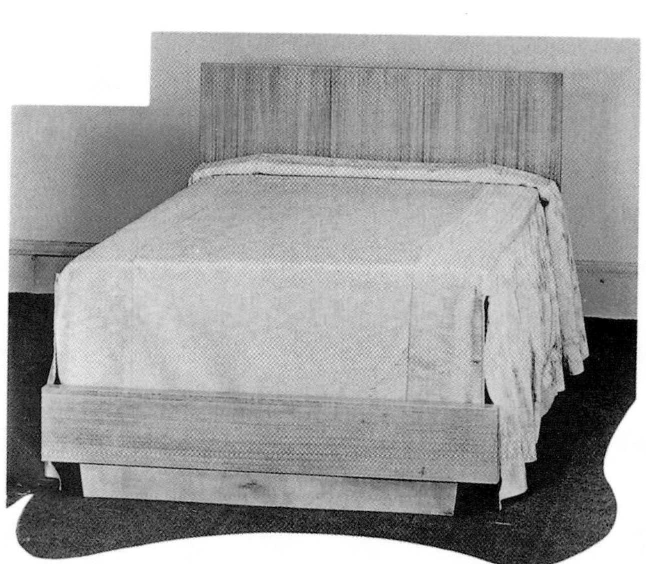

No. 4141 Bed
4' 6" or 3' 3" Head 35" Foot 10"

No. 4140 Vanity Chair
W 21" D 22" H 25"
2 Yards

Designed by G. Rohde

No. 4135 BEDROOM GROUP

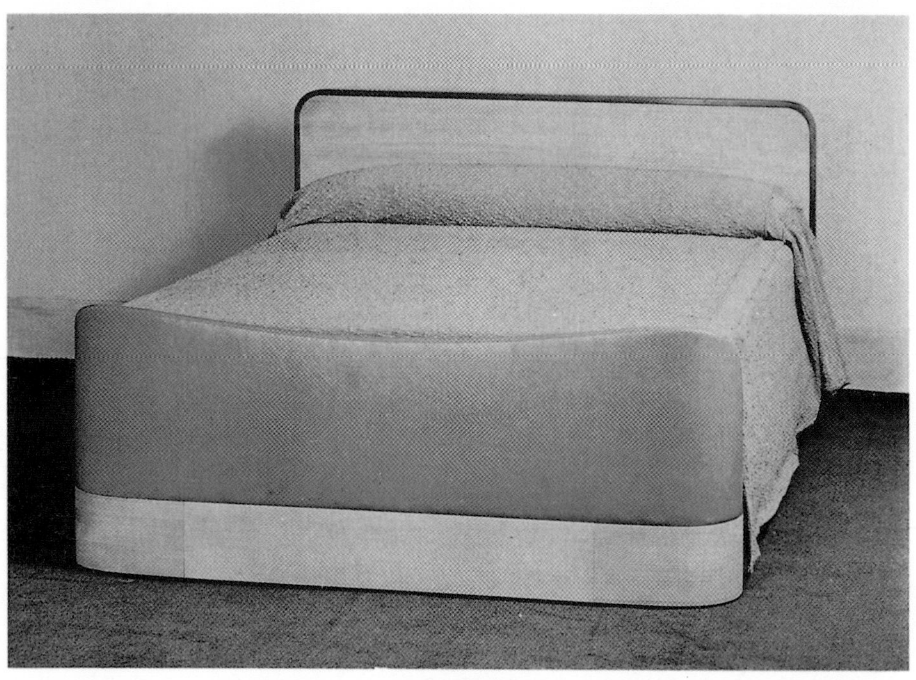

No. 4135 Bed
4' 6" or 3' 3" Head 32" Foot 21½"
No. 4136 Bed is the one with a footboard just like the headboard

No. 4135 Bedside Table
16 x 13" H 25"

No. 4135 Dresser Base
48 x 18" H 33"

No. 4135 Dresser Mirror
30 x 30"

Dressers can be lined up in pairs if wall space is available.

An unusual combination of fine grained Walnut and textured Birch. The Walnut is usually finished in a satiny American Walnut color or in Miller Grey. The Birch is either a plain light brown color or with a white filler in the furring. Thus you get a combination of color and texture. A third texture and color is introduced in the leather cloth used on one of the footends and also on the sides of the Dresser, Chest, and Vanity.

The knobs used are very simple wood usually matching the Walnut in color.

Designed by G. Rohde

No. 4135 BEDROOM GROUP

No. 4135 Chest
36 x 18" H 45"

No. 4135 Bench
16 x 21½" H 16½"

No. 4135 Vanity Base
49½ x 18" H 27"

No. 4135 Vanity Mirror
30 x 30"

Designed by G. Rohde

No. 4144 BEDROOM

PALDAO AND FLAKY WHITE ACER

No. 4144 Bed
4' 6" or 3' 3"
Head 33" Foot 21'

Note the pitched bow of the bed footend and the vanity. Headend perfectly plain and straight. Flaky Acer face with Paldao edges.

No. 4144 Bedside Table
17 x 13" H 25"

A contrast in dark and light and in straight grained and flaky woods.

The pulls are satin brass and satin brass painted lines to indicate the drawer divisions.

No. 4144 Dresser Base
48 x 18" H 32½"

No. 4144 Dresser Mirror
32 x 30"

Designed by G. Rohde

No. 4144 Chest
33 x 18" H 42"

No. 4144 Vanity Base
54 x 19½" H 27"

No. 4144 Vanity Mirror
26 x 26"

No. 4199 Footend Bench
36 x 15" H 16"
1⅔ Yards

Designed by G. Rohde

Value Guide

Of all the decorative arts, furniture is one of the most difficult to price. Condition ranges from the rare perfect piece to those showing degrees of wear and use, because furniture was used in someone's home or office — some pieces more lovingly than others. Prices are understandably affected by condition, including restoration. In addition, each region of the country will have a market directed by supply and demand, by individual tastes, and by fashions or trends. In the case of modern furniture, such as these examples by Gilbert Rohde for Herman Miller, the major coastal cities, plus other centers for modernism such as Chicago and Detroit, generally have the largest and most established markets, and perhaps the highest prices. Large European and Japanese cities have also shown keen interest in American modernism. Auctions often help to guide or set prices, but auctions are events, and once the lots are sold, similar examples at future sales may bring very different prices. Even though Rohde designs have already attracted the attention of many collectors and dealers, they are less well known than the classics by other Herman Miller designers, such as Charles and Ray Eames or George Nelson. Although Rohde was a prolific designer, his untimely death meant that his entire oeuvre spanned only about ten years, and most designs were produced for only a few. There are no known records of the quantity produced for any of these Rohde designs.

With this in mind, it is clear that any price guide for modern furniture is apt to be uneven, to say the least, and *neither the author nor the publisher can be responsible for any outcomes from consulting this guide.* The only guarantee about this or any other value guide is that some readers will buy and/or sell outside of the listed range. That's a fact. Our intent is to give a general idea of some typical prices that similar items have recently sold for and might sell for again. It will also help to distinguish the relatively common from the highly desirable pieces. Prices are in United States dollars, and a range is given to account for different secondary market sources. It is assumed that pieces are in excellent original condition with reasonable wear but no damage or significant restoration. Of course, the pristine example in near mint condition should command a higher price, and there is always the "sleeper" that is worth more than its price tag. Those are surprises that all collectors hope to find. In the meantime, I hope that this catalog brings you enjoyment and provides information that can optimize your chances.

1940 Catalog
Original catalog page numbers are used below.

Walnut Living-Dining

pp. 6-7	Chest/Bookcase	$800-1,000
p. 8	Low Cabinet/Bookcase	$500-700
p. 9	Desk	$1,200-1,600
	Bookcase	$600-900

Walnut Living-Dining

p. 10	Console Dining	$800-1,200
	Table	$400-600
	Lamp Table	$400-600
	Drop Leaf	$1,000-1,500
p. 11	Tables	$500-900

Luxury Group Occasional Tables

p. 12		$700-1,000
	3943	$800-1,200

American Ash Group

p. 14	Chest	$1,200-1,600
	Top Unit	$600-800
p. 15	Bookcase	$600-900
	Units	$400-600
p. 16	Tables	$600-800
	Chair	$300-400
p. 17	Desk	$900-1,200
	Tables	$300-400

Walnut Living Room

p. 18	Desk Table	$600-800
	Movable Drawer	$400-600
	Coffee Table	$300-400
	Bookcase	$500-700

Walnut Dining

p. 19	Chair	$300-400
	Chests	$800-1,000
	Tables	$500-700

Walnut Bedroom

p. 20	Bed	$600-800
	Dressing	$1,000-1,200
	Chests	$600-800

Wall Units in East India Laurel

p. 22	Desk	$600-900
pp. 22-23	Bookcases	$600-800
p. 23	Utility Chest	$700-900

Book Shelves, open $400-600
Console Radio $400-500
Utility Chest $400-500

Laurel Living-Dining Tables
p. 24 Console Table $1,000-1,500
Extension Table $700-900

Laurel Occasional Pieces
p. 25 Desk $1,000-1,500
Flat Top Desk $1,300-1,800
Console Table $700-900
Day Bed End $500-700
p. 26 Tables $400-800

Combination Chairs
p. 28 unit $600-900 each
Double Sector $1,000-1,500
p. 29 Flat Chair $600-800
Corner Chair $700-900
Armless Sofa $1,200-1,800
p. 30 Sleep Sofa $1,000-1,400
p. 31 Sofas, 3-seat $1,300-1,800
Sofas, 2-seat $800-1,200
p. 32 3935 Sofa $1,600-2,200
3706 Sofa $1,200-1,500
955 Sofa $1,200-1,500
p. 33 4041 Sofa $1,200-1,500
4042 Sofa $1,600-2,000

Easy Chairs
p. 35 $600-800
3958 $700-900
Ottoman $300-400
p. 36 top row $1,000-1,200
Ottoman $400-600
Bentwood $1,000-1,200
bottom $600-800
p. 37 Easy Chairs $600-900
p. 38 Easy Chairs $600-800
Twin Grouping $1,200-1,800
p. 39 Arm Chairs $500-700
Tables $300-400
Sofa $1,000-1,200

Desk, Bedroom & Dining
p. 40 Chairs $300-$500
4080 Ottoman $300-400
Ottomans $200-250
p. 41 Chairs $300-500
Bench $300-400
Vanity Chair $400-600
p. 42 Side Chairs $300-400
Arm Chairs $300-500
p. 43 Chairs $300-500

Formal Dining Group 3725
p. 44 Chair $300-500
Table $1,200-1,600
p. 45 Buffet $1,800-2,200
Chair $300-500
China $2,000-2,500
Server $1,000-1,200

Walnut with Chrome Base
p. 46 Oval Table $1,500-1,800
Chairs $300-400
p. 47 Buffet $1,600-2,000
Serving Cart $400-600
Chair $300-400
China $1,800-2,500

Walnut Dining Room
p. 48 Table $1,200-1,500
Chair $300-500
p. 49 China $1,400-2,000
Server $400-600
Cart $500-700
Buffet $1,200-1,800

Formal Dining Room
p. 50 Table $600-800
Server $600-800
Buffet $1,000-1,200
p. 51 Chair $300-400
China $1,200-1,400
Buffet $1,000-1,200

No. 3624 Bedroom Group
p.52 Dresser $700-900
Chair $600-800
Bed $800-1,000
Bedside Table $500-600
p. 53 Vanity $1,200-1,600
Ottoman $300-400
Chair $600-800

No. 3630 Bedroom Group
p. 54 Chair $600-800
Chest $1,000-1,200
p. 55 3631 Bed $1,000-1,200
Bed $800-1,000
Vanity $700-900
Bedside Table $400-500

No. 3770 Bedroom Group
p. 56 Dresser Bases $1,000-1,200 each
3784 Chair $700-900
3454 Easy Chair $600-800
Bedside Table $500-600
Bed $1,500-2,000-
p. 57 Vanity & Mirror $2,200-2,700
Ottoman $300-400
Chest $1,800-2,200

No. 3773 Bedroom Group
p. 58 Dresser Bases $1,500-2,000 each
Portable Mirror $200-300
Chest $2,000-2,500
Bed $2,300-2,800
p. 59 Dressing Table $2,500-3,500
Vanity $2,500-3,500
Ottoman $400-500
Bedside Table $700-900

3930 Bedroom Group

p. 60	Dresser Bases	$1,000-1,500 each
	Bedside Table	$300-400
	Bed	$1,000-1,500
p. 61	Vanity	$1,200-1,700
	Bench	$300-400
	Chair	$300-400
	Chest	$1,200-1,500

No. 3910 Bedroom Group

p. 62	Chair	$600-800
	Dressers	$1,800-2,200 each
	Bedside Table	$600-800
	Dresser Mirror	$300-400
	Bed	$1,200-1,500
p. 63	Vanity Chair	$400-600
	Vanity	$2,500-3,000
	Chest	$2,000-2,500

No. 3920 Bedroom Group

p. 64	Bedside Table	$500-700
	Bed	$1,200-1,500
	Dresser	$1,300-1,800
	Mirror	$200-300
p. 65	Chest	$1,300-1,800
	Bench	$300-400
	Chair	$600-800
	Vanity & Mirrors	$2,500-3,500

No. 4010 Bedroom Group

p. 66	Vanity	$1,800-2,500
	Bedside Table	$400-600
	Bed	$1,000-1,200
p. 67	Chair	$500-700
	Chests	$1,000-1,500
	Bed	$900-1,200

No. 4080 Bedroom Group

p. 68	Chests	$1,000-1,200
	Chair	$300-400
	Bed	$900-1,200
p. 69	Beds	$700-900
	Vanity	$1,000-1,400
	Bedside Table	$400-600

Supplement

Paldao Group

pp. 1-3	Cabinets/Cases	$600-900
p. 4	Breakfront	$3,000-4,000
	Bookcase-Desk	$2,500-3,500
	Chairs	$300-600
p. 5	Low Cabinets	$500-700 unit
	Low Utility	$700-900
	Open Shelves	$500-700
	Coffee Table	$700-900
p. 6	Desk	$1,500-2,000
	Single Pedestal	$1,000-1,500
	Chairs	$300-500
pp. 7-8	Compact	$2,300-2,800
	Chairs	$300-400
p. 9	Cabinets	$1,200-1,600
p. 10	Extension	$800-1,200
	Console	$800-1,000
	Drop Leaf	$1,000-1,500
p. 11	Game Table	$700-900
	Nesting	$800-1,000
	Serving	$600-800
	Corner	$600-800
p. 12	Sofa	$1,000-1,200
	Tables	$600-900
p. 13	Coffee Tables	$700-900
	Lamp/End	$500-700
p. 14	Tables	$600-800

Modern Seating

p. 15	Sofa	$800-1,000
	Chairs	$500-700
p. 16	Sofa	$1,200-1,400
	Bench	$300-500
	Chair	$500-800
p. 17	Chairs	$300-500
p. 18	Chair	$700-900

Paldao Dining

p. 19	Table	$1,200-1,400
	Chairs	$300-400
	Buffet	$1,200-1,400
p. 20	China	$2,000-2,500
	Server	$800-1,000

No. 4130 Bedroom

p. 21	Dresser	$600-800
	Lingerete	$400-500
	Bed	$600-800
	Ottoman	$300-400
	Table	$300-400
p. 22	Chest	$600-900
	Vanity	$900-1,200
	Chair	$300-400

No. 4140 Bedroom

p. 23	Dresser	$900-1,200
	Bed	$700-900
	Bench	$300-500
	Table	$400-500
p. 24	Vanity	$2,000-2,500
	Chest	$900-1,200
	Bed	$700-1,000

No. 4135 Bedroom

p. 25	Bed	$700-900
	Dresser	$700-900
	Table	$400-600
p. 26	Chest	$700-900
	Bench	$300-400
	Vanity	$1,500-1,800

No. 4144 Bedroom

p. 27	Bed	$1,000-1,200
	Dresser	$800-1,000
	Table	$300-400
p. 28	Chest	$800-1,000
	Vanity	$1,500-1,800